Seeing Through

the Eighties

Seeing Through the Eighties

Jane
Feuer

Television and Reaganism

BRITISH FILM INSTITUTE

bfi

BFI PUBLISHING

First published in the UK by the
British Film Institute
21 Stephen Street
London W1P 2LN

Published in the United States by
Duke University Press
Box 90660
Durham, NC 27708-0660
USA

British Library Cataloguing-in-Publication Data.
A catalogue record for this book is available
from the British Library.
ISBN 0-85170-598-7

Printed in the United States of America on acid-free paper ∞
Typeset in Minion by Marathon Typography, Inc.

To Kathie for seeing me through the eighties

Contents

Acknowledgments

In the ten or so years I have worked on this book, I have accumulated a number of debts to a number of generous friends and colleagues.

I would like to thank the Society for the Humanities at Cornell University and its then-director, Jonathan Culler, for making me a part of the fabulous 1990–1991 mass culture year fellowships. I especially want to thank the saintly women who staff the A. D. White House—Mary Ahl, Aggie Sirrine, and Linda Allen—for help way beyond what was expected.

Of my fellow fellows who resided at Cornell that year, I need to single out Simon Frith, who put this project in order for me and helped me think of the title (and told me I *could not* use the word "postmodernism" in the title). I want to thank Constance Penley for telling me that what I was really talking about was modernism and Laura Mulvey for being shocked by her first exposure to American television. Alex Doty, Rachel Bowlby, and Bill Gibson all read my bad drafts and made suggestions. I would like to thank Karal Ann Marling for designing my fortieth birthday cake and Aggie for baking it. Finally, I would like to thank Jeff Stryker for his prodigious and massive accomplishments without which the year would have been just as stimulating but not as much fun.

I owe a great debt to Robert Thompson for opening his archive to me and visiting with me in Ithaca.

The A. C. Nielsen Company, Marissa Piesman, Leonard Heller, and Tony Costa all provided information to me directly and generously.

I want to thank Matthew Tinkcom, Amy Villarejo, and Joy Fuqua for reading the manuscript and telling me it was worth finishing (and for giving me an intellectual second wind during our years together in Pittsburgh).

My colleagues at Pitt, Jonathan Arac and Eric Clarke, made comments that allowed me to revise the manuscript a little bit more than I had intended.

Ken Wissoker, my editor at Duke, believed in the project from the beginning and waited patiently for the manuscript to be delivered. I'm glad to have him as a friend.

Finally, I need to acknowledge the contribution of my partner, Kathie Ferraro, without whom I never could have finished the footnotes and without whom I'm nothing.

Introduction:

The Relationship

between Politics and Television

in the Reagan Era

The year 1981 marked the inauguration of Ronald Reagan as president of the United States; it also marked the debuts of the television serial *Dynasty* and the cable TV service MTV. Looking back, one wonders: which was the cause and which was the effect? Were the new kinds of TV programs functions of Reaganist politics, or was Reagan's election a function of television's role in the "society of the spectacle"? This book will attempt to answer such questions, but the reader should be warned at the outset that the answer will not consist of a simple yes or no, a simple reaffirmation of some kind of unidirectional causal relationship between politics and television. Both *Dynasty* and MTV could be said to be symptoms of the Reagan age—the former in its obsession with the supply-side aristocracy, the latter with its transformation of U.S. network television's linear narrative structure into a postmodern concern with images as images. But neither was really a reflection of an eighties Zeitgeist in any simple way. We can't say that Reaganism as a politically dominant ideology caused the aesthetically superstructural phenomenon of *Dynasty* to happen or that a change in the technological "base" of television—the emergence of cable TV—directly caused MTV to emerge. One could equally well argue that the narrative form *Dynasty* epitomized—the prime-time continuing melodramatic serial—communicated the aura of the eighties as much as any political event, or that MTV and the other technological innovations of the 1980s were a function of deregulation and thus an offshoot of the hegemony of the Republican Party.

Reagan himself, as many have argued, was as much an image as anything else on TV during his presidency. In retrospect, it is clear that he was the ultimate media-constructed image of the times and that the fantasies of unlimited wealth and unlimited visual pleasure that came into office with him were, somehow, the realities of the era. Behind all the images lay only the economic bottom line for which all the images were superstructures. One might say that 1980s culture was financed by imaginary money (junk bonds) in the same way that Reagan was an imaginary president. Even if the 1987 stock market crash and recession brought us out of this particular economic fantasy of the eighties, the era could not be said to have been fantastic in the sense of being unreal, for if watching TV in the eighties taught us anything, it was that the most ephemeral images are capable of real political effect.

Indeed, I will argue that leftists would have done as well to study TV as anything other ideological manifestation during the Reagan presidency if they wanted to understand the relationship between image and "reality" in the postmodern era. But most left intellectuals have yet to appreciate the ideological complexity and contradictory politics of U.S. television. They prefer to study films, because the cinema, as I shall show, remains more culturally respectable than television and not for the most politically correct reasons either. I would maintain, and this book will argue, that television was a more significant medium ideologically and a more artistic medium aesthetically during the 1980s than was Hollywood film. If the emblematic films of the period represented a masculine fantasy of hard bodies and a hard political line (Jeffords 1994), television in the eighties, I will argue, was both more feminized and more ideologically complex.

If the decade was populated by "fictionalized" figures—from Blake Carrington all the way to Ronald Reagan—these fictions had political effectivity in shaping the popular consciousness of the decade; however the relationship between image and reality was not one of simple cause and effect. I will argue that just as TV images could not be said to have caused the eighties, neither could the eighties be said to have produced the images as a simple reflection of the times. Rather, I hope to complicate a base/superstructure model according to which Reaganomics produced, say, the TV series *Dynasty* in a unidirectional manner with a more complex and bidirectional model in which Reaganomics and *Dynasty* are viewed as mutually causing and mutually effecting each other.

Mediating between the economy as a whole and its images of desire was an entire industry that we might call "U.S. network television," an industry whose era was coming to an end during the period I am analyzing. Thus the eighties were both typical of the ongoing relationship between television and politics in America and atypical of that relationship. The period was typical in that politics and entertainment were deeply interwoven but atypical in that network television during the eighties entered into a crisis from which it has yet to emerge. The eighties could be said to have been the end of the era of American network television as we had known it from the 1950s, and like many twilight periods in the history of art and entertainment forms, TV's greatest aesthetic achievements occurred during that crisis and as a result of that crisis.

According to a 1990 retrospective analysis of the television industry, "in the 1980s . . . the fragile foundation on which U.S. television had been constructed began to disintegrate," in terms of its "least common denominator" strategies and "centralized organization." The author of this study, J. Fred MacDonald (1990, p. 221), considers the following facts about the explosion of new technologies during the Reagan era:

— the videocassette recorder (time shifting) was present in 4 percent of U.S. households in 1982, 60 percent in early 1988
— according to Nielsen figures for the first quarter of 1988, each month the average VCR household made 14.1 recordings and watched 16.9 recordings
— the electronic remote control device allowed "zapping" or fastforwarding through ads and "zipping" or "grazing"—jumping from one channel to another
— other new technologies included videodisc, camcorder, video games, and home computers
— PPV (pay per view) reached about one-fifth of all wired households by 1989
— cable penetration increased from 17.1 percent in 1978 to 57.1 percent in 1989
— the people meter was introduced in 1987
— deregulation (the notion that the marketplace should determine programming) was championed by Mark Fowler and Dennis Patrick, the Federal Communications Commission (FCC) chairmen appointed by Reagan. (1990, p. 221)

What is being described here is a shift from a *broad*casting strategy to one of *narrow*casting, at least within certain audience segments. According to a *TV Guide* survey, "There's no question that the remote control switch revolutionized the way we watched TV in the '80s." The survey found that 75 percent of viewers had remote control, and of those 30 percent said they try to watch two or more shows at once—either occasionally or most of the time. Thirty-seven percent said they liked to flip around the dial rather than tune in for a specific program (Lachenbruch 1990, p. 13). At the same time that some viewers were being granted more control over the apparatus, advertisers were being given more control over the demographics they could target. By 1990, then, the entire U.S. television apparatus had undergone a sea change. Technologically, at least for the upscale segments of the audience, television had been transformed. But an apparatus consists of both a technology and the viewing subjects of that technology. This book will argue that the eighties represented a transformation in subjectivity for television as well as a transformation of technology.

Neither John Fiske nor Jean Baudrillard

Such periodizing also resolves certain problems inherent in theories of the media seemingly as disparate as those of international television critic John Fiske and French social/media theorist Jean Baudrillard. I am thus opposed both to the ahistoricism of Jean Baudrillard's concept of resistance and to the totalizing endorsement of the subordinate resisting reader in John Fiske. Within cultural studies, Fiske's work on television reception was widely influential during the eighties in shifting the emphasis away from analyses of how texts position the viewer and toward what the viewer does with the text. Fiske championed the "subordinate" decoder of television images as a type of resisting reader. The conclusion to his book *Television Culture* provides us with a good summary of Fiske's position:

> This brings us to the relationship between entertainment and politics. These are two separate cultural domains which, in Althusserian terms, are relatively autonomous though overdetermined. The resistive readings and pleasures of television do not translate directly into oppositional politics or social action. Relatively autonomous cultural domains do not relate to each other in simple cause and effect terms. But the absence of a direct political effect does not preclude a more general political effectivity. . . . Resistive reading practices that assert the power of the subordinate in the process of representation and its subsequent pleasure pose a direct challenge to the power of capitalism to produce its subjects-in-ideology. The way that people understand themselves and their social relations is part of the social system itself. Any set of social relations requires a set of meanings to hold it in place, and any set of social meanings has to be produced by, and in the interests of, a group or a formation of groups situated within a social system of power relations. (Fiske 1987, p. 326)

While I find little to object to here, and indeed in many ways see this book as an attempt to historicize Fiske's formulation of the relationship between politics and entertainment, I do find one term of this formulation troubling. The term is not, as one might suspect, "resistive," although I have a somewhat different sense of that term, but rather, it is "subordinate." For under Reaganism, there is a sense in which just about every social group was "subordinate" to a dominant white conservative male power block. Given this hegemonic situation, whom should we include in the "subordinate" group that, in theory at least, offers resistive reading practices to the varying forms of Reaganite ideology delineated in this book? Since I intend to show that elements of critique emerge from yuppie culture and that almost all women may have proven to be resistive readers (and since in the United States almost all television is aimed at women), in what sense can we theorize these groups as "subordinate" without rendering the term so broad as to be meaningless? What happens when the interests of one subordinate group (say, gay men) conflict with the interests of another in a particular social formation (say, white working-class men)? In addition, I intend to show that not all "resistive readings" are necessarily pleasing to leftist media critics. Indeed, under the hegemony of Reaganism, many radically "resistive" readings may be said to veer toward the right. In that case, what kind of "political effectivity" do these readings have?

Although Baudrillard's essays on the media were published earlier in France, he was taken up by U.S. media theorists as the 1980s pessimistic interpretation of the same data that McLuhan saw as the "global village" during happier times. Ironically (for he is totally lacking in Fiske's populism), Baudrillard also popularized a theory of the resisting masses, but without the sense of social agency that Fiske's subordinate decoder was said to possess. For Baudrillard the media are postmodern in their emblematic status for the "implosion" of meaning. Baudrillard's whole concept of the silent majority and the masses depends on an older idea of the narcotizing effects of television consumption now articulated in terms of a fashionable postmodernism that defines resistance by the refusal of meaning on the part of the masses. Television is central for Baudrillard (1983a, p. 43) because he conceives of postmodernism (although he doesn't use the term) as a global and totalizing "structure of feeling"—to use Raymond Williams's term—characterized by the implosion of meaning in the masses.

I believe that both Baudrillard's "silent majorities" intent on spectacle and Fiske's resistant "subordinate" decoders can best be read as different attempts at theorizing the Reaganite cultural formation. Both theories deal with the relatively powerless position of the viewer vis-à-vis the production of television texts in the United States. This ongoing fact when combined with the hegemony of the Right during the Reagan/ Thatcher era produced theories of television that empowered readers either to make meanings from the television given them (Fiske) or to refuse to accept meanings in the television given them (Baudrillard). In either case, resistance takes the form of a generalized stance toward the reception of the image. The shift during the eighties from theories of the text to theories of the audience is symptomatic of an era in which left intellectuals felt helpless to influence ideology through production. But simply to assert that negotiated and oppositional decodings are always already being made will not transform an entire apparatus. Perhaps the quietism of the eighties, a period during which reading practices may well have been more resistive than mainstream politics, laid the groundwork for the (admittedly brief) turn to the left in the 1992 elections. But this formulation can only be valuable within a specific historical and cultural situation; it does not constitute a global, over-arching theory of the television apparatus for all time.

Television and Postmodern Art

In this way I hope to retain Fredric Jameson's sense of postmodernism as an historical period, while rendering it more specific and considering the possibility of an uneven development between postmodern TV and other forms of the postmodern. There may be no postmodernism in general, but there may be a postmodern television or a postmodern architecture.

Television presents a further problem for theorists of the postmodern in literature and architecture in that TV is not "post"-anything. There was no modernist TV. No T. S. Eliot, no Stravinsky, no Mies van der Rohe. Despite its prefix, postmodern TV is not something that came after modernist television; for television, once it had displaced film for the title, was the great "other" of modernism. It is difficult to conceive of broadcast television as a modernist art movement, because the conceptualization of television by intellectuals in the United States keeps it firmly within the boundaries of "commodified" mass culture. It was easier for theorists of postmodernism to view video art as the modernist art movement that deconstructs the language of television; in this way postmodern video art could be defined as a form of video that is critical of the language of broadcast video (television). Dara Birnbaum's video art provides the textbook example of this process.[1] In works consisting of looped images from TV shows such as *Wonder*

Woman and *General Hospital*, she takes absurd moments from television and repeats them over and over again against soundtracks that emphasize the incongruity of the context. Although apparently critical in intent, the work was criticized for its easy adaptability to TV commercials and digital graphics, a critique that can always be made if one begins from an assumption that television represents "commodification" but independent video represents "art." But to cite the postmodernity of independent video does not answer the question of the postmodernity of the dominant form of broadcast television.

Both Jean Baudrillard and E. Ann Kaplan do take mainstream television as the model for postmodernism. But they do so on a formalist basis not correlated to any specific historical shifts in subjectivity, culture, or ideology. In her book on MTV, Kaplan considers MTV in general as postmodern, while using the term "postmodern" for a subcategory of music videos as well (1987). For her, postmodernity involves creating unstable subject positions that fall outside of the usual categories. Thus Devo's "Whip It" becomes a text that destabilizes the male gaze rather than one falling solidly within this "sexist" category. Kaplan does not discuss whose reading this is. Nor is it clear how one gets from the formal instability of the video to the progressive reading of its politics, especially if, as Kaplan argues, the target audience for such videos are hip adolescent males. As Simon Frith and Howard Horne have argued, "What makes pop videos post-modern is not their 'exploding signifiers' but their equation of art and commerce: their aesthetic effect can't be separated from their market effect; the desires they address can't be realized except in exchange" (Frith and Horne 1987, p. 168).

By thus historicizing postmodern TV, we can see that its postmodernity correlates to the development of the Reaganite cultural formation, while its specific "artistic" products can be viewed as symptomatic of that formation, yet at the same time critical of it. For Linda Hutcheon the postmodern attitude is one of "complicitous critique," a duality not shared by television, which she finds to be totally complicitous with neoconservatism and thus lacking the critical edge she locates in postmodern literature and photography (1989, p. 10). Yet, as I will argue throughout this book, Hutcheon's "complicitous critique," now re-emerges as a characteristic of certain forms of so-called neoconservative culture. This book will argue that in defining postmodern art as "complicitous critique," theorists of the postmodern were inadvertently elevating certain television programs to art status. For the term "complicitous critique," useful as I find it to my project, also needs to be historicized. In each chapter of the book I will be asking: critical of whom?

complicitous with what? In the final chapter, for example, I argue that, as a postmodern TV program, *Dynasty* challenges our received ideas about what an oppositional text might be and even of how opposition occurs in a seemingly hegemonic era. But *Dynasty* was not alone in this, as I will attempt to demonstrate.

Long before Raymond Williams tried to zap channels in a San Francisco hotel room and thus came up with the concept of "flow" (Williams 1974, p. 71), U.S. television narratives were characterized by interruption and fragmentation. While the term "flow" does capture the lack of closure of American television, it does not really describe its fragmented quality, the quality said to produce a postmodern attention span in our students. I earlier referred to this quality of broadcast TV— what Raymond Williams really observed when he noticed the "flow" of American television—as "segmentation without closure" (Feuer 1983, p. 15). With the technological advances of the 1980s, these qualities have been exacerbated in a form I will call "cable flow." The penetration of cable, remote control, and multiple source input represented the economic and technological impetus for what one might refer to as "postmodern TV." As an aesthetic category, postmodern TV does not represent a break with a prior category but rather an intensification of previous structures and practices. Broadcast flow becomes cable flow. Postmodern TV is a function of cable in terms of both the cable flow channels and the way cable forced the networks to offer more innovative programming in the later 1980s, geared to the yuppie, TV-literate baby boomers.[2] Cable flow thus represents an intensification of certain practices of broadcast flow. If U.S. broadcast TV is characterized by planned interruptions of programming, then cable channels have instituted a flow that denies the boundaries between commercial and program. If U.S. broadcast TV allowed for channel switching, then cable flow allows for zipping, zapping, and channel surfing. If certain network morning shows are designed for intermittent viewing, then cable flow gives us entire services designed for the grazing viewer.

Cable flow services are not critical in and of themselves, as certain notions of the flow of MTV have suggested. Simon Frith delivers a scathing critique of certain views of MTV as the ultimate postmodern artifact, arguing that, if one attempts to define the postmodernism of MTV by its formal features, one winds up citing its most commodified side—for the constant flow of MTV derives from top forty radio (1988, p. 206). Baudrillard follows McLuhan in assuming that the impact of the television medium is due entirely to its form, regardless of particular contents, so that, for example, it doesn't matter if you watch *Miami*

Vice or *Dragnet*. Simply considering MTV as a new kind of flow leaves it as just another avant-garde art movement. We haven't correlated it to popular subjectivity or political periodization.

Linda Hutcheon has written that "most television, in its unproblematized reliance on realist narrative and transparent representational conventions, is pure commodified complicity, without the critique needed to define the postmodern paradox" (1989, p. 10). She does not seem to understand that what is postmodern is television's textuality generally, not individual TV "artworks" conceived as breaking with transparent conventions of narrative. Her claim about realist narrative is, quite simply, untrue; and the most naive regular TV viewer is more qualified to judge this than the more sophisticated—but televisually naive—literary critic.

From its earliest days (e.g., *The George Burns and Gracie Allen Show*, 1950–1958; and *Gidget*, 1965–1966), but especially from the late 1970s onward, television has been relentlessly self-reflexive. Whether this self-consciousness and obsessive self-referencing constitute a critique of the television apparatus in the modernist/Marxian sense of the term is more debatable, yet I find that the sheer proliferation of programs that exhibit either self-reflexivity or a parodic impulse in 1980s TV bears its own kind of weight for the argument that a postmodern form of complicitous critique was operating throughout the eighties on American network and cable television. Models for a new kind of programming for baby boomers emerged in the 1970s in the form of the late-night parody shows *Saturday Night Live* (1975–present) and *SCTV Comedy Network* (syndicated 1977–1981; NBC, 1981–1983; Cinemax, 1983). *SCTV Comedy Network* went so far as to critique the entire concept of television flow in its own formal structure as a pseudo–TV network complete with commercials.

The tradition of confining the postmodernist sensibility to late night (when, presumably, middle America was sleeping) continued with *Late Night with David Letterman* (1982–1993), a program even the *New York Times* referred to as "an absurdist parody of mass culture" (30 June 1984, p. 7). Among other fringe programs, *Pee Wee's Playhouse* has often  been cited as a postmodern children's show; certainly the playhouse contains the most extreme examples of postmodern design to appear on TV. And the entire cable service *Nick at Nite* might be cited as postmodern for its rewriting of TV history—taking those very naive representational programs and postmodernizing them in a different context, exactly what postmodern architecture does to the history of buildings. Our prototypical cable flow service, MTV, has been described by E. Ann Kaplan (1987) and others (for example, Andrew Goodwin 1992, pp. 156–181) as "postmodern." Music videos, while themselves fully commodified, often critique commodification (e.g. Dire Straits' music video *Money for Nothing*). An entire two-hour flow of MTV was dubbed "postmodern videos" to account for those outside of an apparently complicitous norm. Furthermore MTV's narrative conventions are nonrealist, and individual programs broadcast on the service such as *The Young Ones* and *Remote Control* are very decentered. Even a single series such as *Dynasty* (in its encouragement of camp decodings) may be considered double-edged at the level of reception. Considered together, the percentage of broadcast and cable television that could be considered "pomo" takes on the impetus of a trend, perhaps even a period in the history of the medium. And that period begins in the 1980s.

An overall distinction between a good (deconstructive) postmodernism and a bad (neoconservative) postmodernism is difficult to make at the level of textual analysis, especially when it is assumed that the avant-garde is always good and the mass media always bad. In this sense, TV is like architecture; we inhabit its postmodernism in our daily lives without necessarily responding to it as an art movement. And yet, cumulatively, we may assume it to have an impact—from the pedimented facades of fast food restaurants to the endless flow of the cable services—but whether that impact is complicitous with or critical of a dominant Reaganite ideology no amount of textual analysis can determine. Indeed we may want to conclude that postmodern TV—like several other postmodernisms—deconstructs the very oppositions between commodity and art, complicity and critique.

Both Stuart Hall and Kevin Phillips

Although leftist and conservative analysts placed a very different value on Reaganism and analyzed its hegemony in very different languages, they seemed in remarkable agreement both in acknowledging the popular success of Reaganite hegemony and in attributing that success to forms of populism. It is interesting to compare Republican political commentator Kevin Phillips's analysis of the "New Right" in the United States (1983) with Stuart Hall's leftist analysis of Thatcherism (1988) as the hegemonic political ideologies of the eighties. As Hall has written regarding Thatcherism, the present crisis (of the Left) may be characterized in terms of Gramsci's "war of position": "The nature of a 'success' in a war of position has to be thoroughly reworked. Victory does not consist of the appearance, newly minted, of some total 'world view,' or some wholly evolved alternative 'social order,' which has been slowly maturing, like a good cheese, in the vaults of the left, to be brought out at the right moment and propelled on to the field of struggle" (1988, p. 130). Thatcher, in contrast, understood how to galvanize popular ideology during the eighties via a strategy Hall labels "authoritarian populism" (1988, pp. 138–146). Authoritarian populism refers to the winning of popular consent to the authority of the Thatcherite regime, associating social democracy with the power bloc and Mrs. Thatcher with "the people." This has been achieved by "fracturing" traditional popular ideologies, invoking "themes of crime and social delinquency, articulated through the discourses of popular morality," that "touch the direct experience, the anxieties and uncertainties of ordinary people" (pp. 138–146).

Such a description bears a remarkable resemblance, in descriptive if not in evaluative terms, to Kevin Phillips's depiction of the "New Right" under Reaganism during the same moment. Phillips believes the New Right was more important ideologically than the neoconservatives because it was a mass movement of middle-class fundamentalists (1983, p. 47). That is to say, neoconservatism was the political ideology of intellectuals of the Reaganite formation; populism, the ideology of the masses. In a chapter on the failure of liberal economics and the populist response, Phillips writes that conservative theory puts the blame for the last two decades of inflation on government—either on the state-orchestrated growth of the money supply or on the growth of the public sector/welfare state and its impact on incentive and productivity. He feels that tax revolt is more populist than conservative, given that tax revolts had previously come from the left (1983, pp. 123–124). Phillips also believes that to get low-middle-income populist constituencies to go for the elitist parts of Reaganism, it had to appeal to a "set of cultural and nationalistic themes." Thus "post-industrial or communications-age 'populism' may wind up rather authoritarian in substance, anti-government rhetoric nonwithstanding" (pp. 132–133). Populism in the 1980s and 1990s appears as a volatile ideology that rapidly swings to the right and left of center within a short time span. This book will describe a similar toggling in the television of the same period.

Television and Reaganism

If Reaganomics made Reagan early in the 1980s, it is tarnishing his image in the 1990s with the death of the yuppie, the end of the aristocracy of wealth, and the inability to sustain the mythology of good times. Or did Reaganism signal the end of ideology in the old sense? Behind all the images were there simply more images? In seeing *through* the eighties (i.e., in demystifying the period), perhaps it is the seeing that was all-important; perhaps we were living in a hall of mirrors that was not in any way transparent.

It was also said of the 1960s that television was crucial to politics, but the metaphors used to describe the influence of TV involved bringing reality *in*, as with Michael J. Arlen's "living-room war" (1969) and Todd Gitlin's "the whole world is watching" (1980). What is interesting about descriptions of TV and politics in the 1980s is their focus on the way we used TV to keep reality *out*, as in Haynes Johnson's "sleepwalking through history" (1991). Arguably the mass media were even more influential in constructing (not just reflecting) the imaginary decade of the 1980s. The media didn't exactly cause the 1980s to happen, nor did the 1980s exactly cause emblematic shows like *Dynasty* and *thirtysomething*; rather, television and Reaganism formed mutually reinforcing and interpenetrating imaginary worlds.

This is why, in opening up the connection between television and Reaganism, I have ignored the obviously ideological components of 1980s TV in favor of what may at first appear to be trivial entertainment forms. This book does not focus on the news, on Christian broadcasting, on talk shows, or even on crucial Reaganite sitcoms such as *Cosby* and *Family Ties*. I am more interested in the programs we used to *avoid* dealing with the economic and social realities of the times than in these important but less contradictory TV genres. That is why *Seeing Through the Eighties* focuses on a contradiction in Reaganite ideology that I believe also permeates certain symptomatic television contents and forms of the period. According to Kevin Phillips, Reaganomics stands for "a curious mix of populism and elitism." It is populist in that "it opposes an expansion of government power, regulatory and fiscal interference with the enterprising public"; elitist in that "it espouses tax relief aimed at upper-income brackets, believes in 'trickle down' economics, and exalts the gifted and entrepreneurial over the common man" (1983, pp. 131–132). I believe these contradictions were played out in the television of the period. Seeing through the eighties involves seeing through TV at a number of levels.

Although this book is not comprehensive in the sense of covering all types of television, it tries to cover the entire spectrum of the Reaganite symbolic universe—from the New Right to the very rich to the yuppies as they are represented on TV. But this is not a content analysis. I am also convinced that the overall *forms* of eighties TV are symptomatic of Reaganism. The idea of an ideology of form comes up in the discussion of the narrative structure of the made-for-TV social problem movie, in the discussion of the ensemble cast serial melodrama as the dominant form of the decade, and in the discussion of the postmodernity of the introduction of modernist art discourses into American television during the eighties. Of course, political ideologies do not come to us directly. In the case of television, an entire industry mediates between TV images and cultural and political images. Television economics, although certainly capitalist, were not entirely Reaganomic. Whereas Reagan had at least to pretend to view Americans as citizens—or voters—the TV industry conceptualizes Americans entirely as a market—or as during the late eighties, a number of discrete markets. Since for most of the decade TV was not considered the ideal medium for selling elite goods, it always had to reach for a broader audience than yuppies, and it could never address itself to the very rich. Images of the very rich were always sent out to a mass audience. But within that mass audience, certain subcultural groups were able to interpret those images for their own ends. My discussion of the reception of *Dynasty* by gay men and straight women grapples with the difficult issue of resistance to Reaganism through television. If I do not discuss the reception of TV programs by groups totally disenfranchised in the eighties—poor blacks, the homeless, the elderly—it is not because I consider them insignificant, but rather because I am interested in groups the industry tried to address.

In different chapters of *Seeing Through the Eighties*, the elitist/populist split is shown to color a different part of the political spectrum or a different form of television. Chapter 1 deals with populism as it informs a typically eighties brand of made-for-TV movie. Beginning in 1979, a wave of made-for-TV movies known in the trade as "trauma dramas" appeared on the U.S. airwaves, on all three networks and with a variety of creative personnel. The eighties version of the "sociological film" or "public service drama" resolved the traumas of the American family in a rejuvenation of public institutions by the people, the same promise that got Reagan elected. Chapter 1 shows how, under Reaganism, even populism took on an elitist cast in its emphasis on the figure of a charismatic individual who went on to transform the welfare state bureaucracy into a grass-roots New Right utopia. The frustration expressed in these films reflects the real social frustrations of the times, but their political inflection is subject to debate—for the new populism as embodied in these films is not unambiguously right wing in sentiment.

Whereas the first chapter focuses on the populist majority, the second and third chapters deal with a tiny but significant fraction of the Reagan formation—the yuppies. The yuppie was as much a media construct as Ronald Reagan himself. The yuppie was the other side to the populism of the decade; the year of the yuppie (1984) was also the year of Reagan's reelection, of Diana Vreeland's Yves Saint Laurent retrospective at the Met, of the rise of *Dynasty* to the top of the TV charts, of *Miami Vice*. George Orwell was wrong: 1984 would come to represent an orgy not of totalitarianism but of consumerism. And yet the yuppies were not the Reagans. Nor were they an aristocratic holdover, a dynasty, or even a ruling class. Rather, the yuppies were a fragment of the baby boomers or of the professional-managerial class that seized the imagination of a larger segment of the population to become a marketing icon; in no way part of the trend to moral conservatism, they represented the rediscovery of success by a formerly rebellious generation. And they were scorned. For "yuppie" was always a term you applied to somebody else. It was not a promising concept for the mass-market orientation of the television industry. Chapters 2 and 3 examine the ways in which the TV industry dealt with these contradictions surrounding the yuppie image.

Due to the influx of capital into certain culture industries—specifically the design industries, broadcast television, and the culinary arts—during the 1980s, one could argue that an artistic renaissance of sorts took place in precisely those art forms most dependent on capital for their very expression/realization. In an ideologically elitist period, it makes sense that architecture, interior design, gourmet cooking, restaurant culture, and broadcast television would flourish, at least economically. What I want to argue is that these art forms flourished aesthetically as well. Thus chapter 4 deals with the aesthetics of yuppie ideology aka postmodern art. During the eighties, postmodernism came to TV under the guise of modernism. This chapter will show how programs such as *thirtysomething*, *Moonlighting*, and *Max Headroom* emerged as a new form of art television via their construction as art discourse—a construction that was wholly postmodern in spirit.

Prior to the 1980s, serial melodrama was overwhelmingly a daytime

form; the only successful prime-time example was *Peyton Place* (1964–1969), the film version of which belonged to the 1950s Hollywood melodrama. Although during the 1970s there seemed to be no equivalent on prime-time television to the film melodramas of the 1950s recently rescued from obscurity by film theorists, during the Reagan era, domestic melodrama encroached upon the domain of the sitcom and the cop show. In an uncanny conjuncture, *Dynasty* ran almost exactly as long as the Reagans occupied the White House. By January 1991, *Dynasty* producer Douglas Cramer was quoted as saying, "The Reagans are out of the White House, and John [Forsythe] and Joan [Collins] are out of the mansion. . . . You only have to look at the papers to see where we are in terms of the recession and the homeless" (Zurawick 1991, p. 6).

Chapter 5 details the rise of the ensemble cast serial melodrama as the dominant form of television during the 1980s, showing how it became the ideal form for exploring the political contradictions of the decade. There is a parallel here to the populism of the made-for-TV movies discussed earlier, a populism whose inflection to the right rather than toward a socialistic reading depended on numerous factors outside the formal constraints of the films themselves. Narrative forms in themselves cannot structure the ideologies of an era, yet narrative forms—especially the very simple one of the TV sitcom—do have expressive limitations, and, in the case at hand, one can correlate a shift in the dominant narrative form of American network television with a shift in sensibilities outside the text. It would seem that the multiplication of social contradictions in the 1980s could not be expressed within the boundaries of the situation comedy. This is not to say, as many have argued, that the new serials represent a turning away from social concerns. The emergence of the melodramatic serial in the 1980s represents a radical response to and expression of cultural contradictions. Whether that response is interpreted to the Right or to the Left is not a question the texts themselves can answer. Instead one must examine the reception of a program such as *Dynasty* by audiences during the period of its greatest popularity.

This is what chapter 6 sets out to do. For a moment in the mid-1980s the television serial *Dynasty* ceased being merely a program and took on the proportions of a major mass cultural cult. This phenomenon has been widely interpreted as representing the acquiescence of the mass audience to the Reaganite ideology of greed and asocial avarice. But the response of the so-called masses to *Dynasty* was far more complex than a mere affirmation of the worst of Reaganism. This chapter will analyze the response to *Dynasty* as a complex phenomenon that has aspects both of commodification from above and subcultural activation from below. For although *Dynasty* was the number one rated program overall in the 1984–1985 TV season, its fans were not simply a mass audience. Rather, they were clustered in two quadrants of a male/female; gay/straight combinatoire—that is to say, the two groups that became obsessed with *Dynasty* in the mid-1980s were gay men and heterosexual women. This chapter explores what these audiences did with *Dynasty*.

The eighties are emerging more and more as an incredibly hegemonic period; and yet we are also more and more able to sense contradictions that were played out in the culture. Because of the hegemonic politics, we are able to "periodize the eighties" in the sense of seeing that the same phenomena, for example, TV and politics, worked themselves out at different levels.[3] But it is the contradictions that enable us to see what Stuart Hall and others mean when they characterize "hegemony" as a struggle over meanings, a process that is always ongoing even when (as during the mid-eighties) it seems as if one side has won a decisive victory. This is why it is important to look at the meanings under discussion as always being contested. In each chapter, what might be considered a dominant ideology is revealed to be actually a product of a temporary Reaganite victory in the ongoing struggle. It is also crucial to consider the subversive things audiences did with these programs in those cases where evidence exists, as for *Dynasty* or the widespread reaction to *thirtysomething* as the show you love to hate.

I hope to show that underneath the seemingly uniform television culture of the eighties, contradictions abounded. This reading of eighties TV points to the instability of Reaganism as a formation and to the possibility that a better understanding of television could have led to a better understanding of Reaganism by the Left. Perhaps those of us who spent the eighties watching TV could claim to have been the true radicals of the decade—whether for better or for worse, only history can say.

Notes

1 Birnbaum's technique informs Joan Braderman's *Joan Does Dynasty*, analyzed in chapter 6.
2 Cable flow channels is a term I've coined to describe entire cable TV stations that embody the concept of continuous flow that for Raymond Williams defines

American television. I will concentrate on the proliferation of what I call "cable flow services"—cable channels characterized by twenty-four-hour flow that are themselves sung to the rhythm of the remote control. These services include MTV (paradigmatically), the Weather Channel, ESPN, Cable Network News, CNBC, E!, and shopping and fashion services.

3 This is a reference to Fredric Jameson (1988, chapter 9, "Periodizing the 6os," pp. 178–179). Jameson writes:

> Now, this is not the place for a theoretical justification of periodization in the writing of history, but to those who think that cultural periodization implies some massive kinship and homogeneity or identity within a given period, it may quickly be replied that it is surely only against a certain conception of what is historically dominant or hegemonic that the full value of the exceptional— what Raymond Williams calls the "residual" or "emergent"—can be assessed. Here, in any case, the "period" in question is understood not as some omnipresent and uniform shared style or way of thinking and acting, but rather as the sharing of an objective situation, to which a whole range of varied responses and creative innovations is then possible, but always within that situation's structural limits.

1

The Made-for-TV "Trauma Drama":
Neoconservative Nightmare or
Radical Critique?

An Iowa farm wife takes on the U.S. Army after her son is killed by "friendly fire" in Vietnam; a mother battles the legislature to change the drunk driving laws after her daughter is killed; a father gets Congress to tighten the FBI's authority to investigate the murders of children after his son is abducted in a shopping mall; a battered wife, cast aside by numerous human welfare bureaucracies, sets fire to her husband's bed; distraught parents battle the medical establishment to stop treatment of their severely impaired child in a neonatal intensive care unit; parents unable to control their wayward drug-addicted son lock him out of the house. This massive loss of faith by individuals in institutions occurred not only in the courts and homes and hospitals of America during the 1980s, but also on its TV screens. Beginning in 1979, a wave of made-for-TV movies known in the trade as "trauma dramas" appeared on the U.S. airwaves, on all three networks and with a variety of creative personnel (see appendix A). The eighties version of the "sociological film" or "public service drama"[1] resolved the traumas of the American family in a rejuvenation of public institutions by the people, the same promise that got Reagan elected.

Although there existed a long tradition of socially realistic literature and film that mirrored social problems in the dilemmas of families,[2] this group of films seemed peculiarly symptomatic of the popular frustrations that brought Reagan to office and fueled the New Right engine of the 1980s. These films invoked a long tradition of American populism, but gave it an inflection that was specific to the Reagan agenda. According to Kevin P. Phillips, the new conservatism of the Reagan era was not really conservatism, in the classic sense, but rather a manifestation with populist and radical roots: "In many ways, populism, not conservatism, is the electoral force unique to our politics. . . . American populism has gathered force and helped to give ideological direction to the nation when it confronted various historical crossroads" (1983, pp.

xxii). Since Phillips believes that the 1960s and 1970s "are second only to the Civil War and the decade preceding it as a time of national breakdown," it is not surprising that the aftermath of this period should see a populist revival (1983, p.18). Although populism is often associated with agrarian issues, even the author of a book focusing on the agrarian dimension of populism in the popular culture of the 1980s agrees that "the strongest expression of populism in the 1980s is not so much the agrarian issues as the overall disillusionment with politics" (Webster 1988, p. 4). It is precisely this populist and anti-institutional rather than specifically conservative ideology that is manifested in the films that I will analyze in this chapter. I hope to show that the frustration expressed in the films reflects the real social frustrations of the times, but that the political inflection of such frustrations is subject to debate—for the new populism as embodied in these films is not unambiguously right wing in sentiment.

Why should the made-for-TV movie be the televisual form that renders the "center extremist"[3] agenda most clearly? One answer is that it is not. Many forms of television in the eighties expressed frustration with the legal system. The cop show in particular expresses a neoconservative agenda, rife with criminals getting away with murder on legal technicalities based on flawed liberal reasoning. *Hill Street Blues* endlessly invoked this scenario. So did the news—but the news was not supposed to narrativize too much or identify too blatantly with a particular viewpoint. The made-for-TV movie with its tradition of social realism combines the ideology of the cop show with the reality claims of the news. In fact many of these trauma dramas take the form of the docudrama, by definition a narrative representation of "real people" and "real events." So much of the impact of the trauma drama consists in this badge of authenticity—"this really happened to people just like you." In this sense the docudrama represents the inverse of the typical Hollywood fiction film with its inevitable disclaimer: "any resemblance to actual persons living or dead is unintentional." The claims to truth status appear right up front, often reinforced by being read by an intimidating male voice: "The story you are about to see is true. The names of the principal characters and government officials depicted have *not* been changed" (*Adam*, 1983). "On May 3, 1980, Cari Lightner was struck by a drunk driver. The following is based on her true story" (*M.A.D.D.*, 1983). "Farrah Fawcett in a powerful drama torn from today's headlines—based on a true story of a woman trapped in a brutal and violent marriage until the night she struck back" (*The Burning Bed*, 1984). "On March 15, 1982, actress Theresa Saldana was viciously attacked and repeatedly stabbed. She barely survived. This is her story" (*Victims for Victims,* 1984). At times the claim to authenticity approaches the voyeuristic—as when, in *Victims for Victims,* actress Theresa Saldana reenacts her own traumatic knife attack or when in *The Ann Jillian Story* (1988) that actress recreates her own encounter with breast cancer.[4] Even in those trauma dramas that are not docudramas—known tellingly as "fictionalized" versions—the level of topicality implies "truth to life." In *Toughlove* (1985), for example, a fictional family is torn apart by the son's drug habit. The movie's authenticity is affirmed when the parents seek help from the actual organization Toughlove. They too receive a civics lecture indistinguishable from those in docudramas (permissive child rearing has ruined our country—lock your kid out of the house—you have rights too). The fact that even in the "fictionalized" accounts the "problem" may be dealt with after the film by means of what I will call "nonstory" materials lends further authenticity to the trauma. *An Early Frost* (1985), the AIDS trauma drama, is, technically speaking, fictionalized, and yet the trauma dealt with became the subject of followup segments on the news.

A *TV Guide* "Commentary" from 1987 is typical of elitist criticism of the docudrama form. Titled "Danger! Please Don't Mix Facts with Fiction," the article has no trouble with the epistemological questions over which theorists agonize: "Too many people, I fear, think these fictionalized movies are true; too many people, I fear, are forming—and then transmitting—their final impressions of the major social and political events of our time on the basis of fictionalized movies, rather than on the basis of historical fact" (*TV Guide* 1987, p. 12).

Putting aside the author's assurance of the knowability of "facts," I would argue that the nonelite classes have always received their "history" in the form of narrative, making narrative and history mutually reinforcing—the "facts" are made pleasurable through narrative; narrative is made more enlightening through a moralizing discourse. Television's tendency to treat history as narrative is nothing new. In his study of the history of the concept of objectivity in American journalism, Michael Schudson distinguishes between the "story" ideal and the "information" ideal as models for journalism (1978).

Tracing the ascendancy of the *New York Times* in the 1890s as the model for "accuracy" in journalism, Schudson points out that neither of these competing models has a greater claim to the "truth." The story ideal, embodied in the popular newspapers of Pulitzer and Hearst, fulfilled an "aesthetic" function of storytelling, according to an analysis by

George Herbert Mead quoted by Schudson. Here the "consummatory value" of the news is most important. The reporter's object is to get "a story" and to select and frame events into a plot as does any author of narrative fiction. The information ideal—still held up as a standard in the *TV Guide* article I quoted—assumes that "facts" can be presented unframed. According to Schudson: "Rightly or wrongly the information ideal in journalism is associated with fairness, objectivity, scrupulous dispassion. Newspapers which stress information tend to be seen as more reliable than 'story' papers" (1978, pp. 89–90). Schudson goes on to stress the ideological nature of our preference for the informational ideal—showing that, historically, there has always been a strong link between the educated middle class and information, and the middle and working classes and the story ideal. It is from the ideological perspective of just this "educated middle class" that the above-mentioned criticisms of docudrama emanate. Hayden White has suggested that narrative is inherently a *moralizing* form of historical organization (1980, p. 14), and it may be just this moralizing quality that offends critics of docudrama.

Yet the same moralizing tendency makes the docudrama especially well equipped to represent populist ideology. Margaret Canovan sees populism as "a family of related ideas that usually features agrarian radicalism, antielitism or both, and that invariably puts great emphasis on idealizing or mobilizing the people" (quoted in Phillips 1983, p. 32). The agrarian populist movement of the 1890s tended toward collective action with a socialistic impulse, but populism of the Reagan era was individualistic (see Goodwyn 1978). Although it is very difficult to express collectivity on film (whether because of inherent limits of narrative or historical tradition I'm not equipped to argue here), the expression of individual social action became the hallmark of the 1980s docudrama. Collective action, although implied in the films (see below), did not predominate. "The people" are idealized and mobilized through the actions of a charismatic individual, pointing to a contradiction between individualism and antielitism inherent in Reaganite ideology.

This charismatic individual is democratized, however, in a manner separating him or her from the kind of movie-star individualism found elsewhere in 1980s TV and in the White House. If in classical Hollywood narratives, beautiful stars become objects of the gaze, in made-for-TV social problem movies, these same stars consciously uglify themselves (e.g., Farrah Fawcett in *The Burning Bed*; Raquel Welch in *Right to Die*, 1987). We gaze now with morbid fascination rather than lust at faces

bruised or wasted by disease. Even comedienne Carol Burnett is cast against type in *Friendly Fire* (1979), her plainness now exploited for populistic rather than comic gain. Indeed the need *not* to provide visual pleasure is emphasized when actors are cast in the parts of "real people." In *Adam* and its sequel (*Adam: His Song Continues,* 1986), the parts of John and Revé Walsh are filled by the notably average-looking Daniel J. Travanti and JoBeth Williams. The viewer is given a small stab of visual fulfillment near the end of *Adam* when the real Walshes appear—both notably better-looking than the actors who have portrayed them, both indeed appearing by comparison to be "movie stars" just as the actors appeared "real." Indeed John Walsh did become a TV star, currently gracing the small screen in a reincarnation of his real-life role as the vigilante host of *America's Most Wanted.* Ironically, by 1991, Walsh's ruggedly handsome all-American face was far more familiar to the viewing public than that of the more ethnic Travanti.[5]

In order to understand how populism works in these movies, it is useful to examine in detail the 1979 film *Friendly Fire,* arguably the earliest complete example of the type. The opening images of the film invoke the agrarian ideal, reinforced by a printed title: "Iowa, 1969." A young man, Michael Mullen, is spending his last day on the family farm prior to being shipped off to Vietnam; the opening segment of the film emphasizes what his mother will say later on: "My son was a farmer, not a soldier." As if the images of the sunlit land and the amazingly young blond soldier were not enough to establish typicality, the camera soon lingers over a billboard for the nearby town La Porte City, population 2256, "where people count most." Ironically, this image is given under Michael's voice-over reading of letters home from Vietnam. Because we anticipate his death (the film is a docudrama based on a non-fiction book and, besides, *TV Guide* told us it would happen), the first portion of the film seems even more agonizingly slow than its average shot length would indicate. Yet the death occurs only twenty minutes into the three-hour (with ads) docudrama. The purpose of the first twenty minutes is to establish a lingering afterimage of the normal life the Mullens might have had if the trauma of the son's death in Vietnam had not occurred. This pattern of establishing an all-American normality prior to the traumatic event will persist in every film. But it is the trauma that singles out *this* family, and therefore the bulk of screen time is devoted to its aftermath. These films are not about the lost or damaged children, rather they focus on the parents' efforts to redress grievances. This is why the charismatic individual is always the parent, in this case, the stalwart farm wife Peg Mullen, movingly played by Carol Burnett. As the film continues, we watch her (and to a lesser extent her husband) being transformed into what can only be described as a true fanatic. She insists that the word "killed" rather than "died" be inscribed on the tombstone and is relentless in her pursuit of the truth. This parental fanaticism is typical and establishes a prototype for future docudramas such as *M.A.D.D.*, *Adam*, and *Shootdown* (1988). The major portion of the film depicts Peg's attempts to find out what really happened to her son, a "nonbattle" casualty of fire from "friendly" artillery. As she penetrates more and more layers of lies from the army bureaucracy, Peg moves away from her Iowa community and into the center of a national community of antiwar activists, parents of sons killed in Vietnam. In a telling moment, she informs some friends, "I feel closer to all those fathers and mothers who write to us [than to you]." In the process of taking on the army, Peg achieves personhood and even celebrity, but it is a grim sort of fame that alienates her from the agrarian community. As in *Lois Gibbs and the Love Canal* (1982) and *M.A.D.D.* (Mothers Against Drunk Drivers), the ordinary mother finds her voice in the public pursuit of an activism whose motivation is intensely private. Unlike in some of the later films, however, Peg does not mobilize the community behind her until very near the end of the film, when the tide has turned against the war. By the end of the film she seems no less bitter for having learned the truth, and the mood is bittersweet.

It was not until 1983 that the full thrust of the pattern initiated by *Friendly Fire* would be realized in two crucial and remarkably similar TV movies: *M.A.D.D.* and *Adam.*[6] Now, however, several years into the

Reagan administration, the frustration with social institutions that had taken on a populist form has acquired a neoconservative bent. *Friendly Fire*, because it focused on the anti–Vietnam War movement, over by the time the film was made, could inflect its populism in a liberal direction—liberal but not collective. These later films take on the individualistic populism of *Friendly Fire* and the 1982 *Lois Gibbs and the Love Canal*, which were directed at the army and the government, respectively; but now invest the antielitist desire in favor of a New Right agenda for victims' rights that will permeate the made-for-TV movie for the rest of the decade.

In addition, these films stress the triumph of the parents in mobilizing the legal system in favor of victims' rights. They are sagas of idealizing and mobilizing the people, but they retain the focus on the individual effort. By now, however, "the people"—including the implied viewers—are on the side of the parents; it is only the institutions that need to change.

According to Kevin Phillips, the Reagan coalition's regional base consisted of the Sunbelt, the Farm Belt, and the west—"the traditional populist and antielite component of U.S. political geography" (Phillips 1983, p. 15). Strikingly, some of the major populist telefilms occupy the same geographic and ideological landscape. When we move from the anti-Vietnam to the pro-victim paradigm, we shift from the Farm Belt to Sunbelt suburbanites in Florida (*Adam*) and California (*M.A.D.D.*), respectively. This serves to identify the charismatic parent figure with the populist core of America. It reinforces the typicality of the normal family shown to us as if for an object lesson at the beginning of each of these films. Since I am taking *Adam* and *M.A.D.D.* as paradigmatic, I would like to emphasize these two (but also draw on later films) for an analysis of the plot structure of the 1980s made-for-TV populist trauma drama, a structure that will occur in a number of significant made-for-TV movies of the era and reoccur, sometimes with variations, in a significant number of the films:

1. The family represents the ideal and norm of happy American family life.
2. A trauma occurs.
3. The victims/parents seek help through established institutions.
4. The institutions are unable to help them and are shown to be totally inadequate.
5. The victims take matters into their own hands.
6. They join a self-help group or form a grass-roots organization.

7. The new organization is better able to cope with the trauma, often having an impact on established institutions.
8. Normality is restored (however inadequately).

The family represents the ideal and norm of happy American family life. Although this "function" of ideal family life occurred in *Friendly Fire,* the joyousness of farm life was undercut by the heavy atmosphere caused by the son's impending departure.[7] In *M.A.D.D.* this function is also present but in so abbreviated a form one could almost miss it: the pretitle sequence shows two typical girls walking home from school; at the moment of impact, Cari turns as the frame freezes; there is a zoom in and fade to black as Cari Lightner is struck by the drunk driver's car. It is *Adam*, then, that perfectly captures this brief moment of life before the trauma. The family is gathered round the sunlit suburban kitchen as the endearingly cute Adam Walsh sings an aria; the strains of "Figaro" will haunt his father ever after. Even the scene of Adam's abduction—a suburban shopping mall—appears more normal than menacing.

A trauma occurs. But the normal atmosphere is not allowed to persist for more than the first segment of the trauma drama: Adam is kidnaped and murdered; Cari Lightner is the victim of vehicular manslaughter; Francine Hughes is beaten repeatedly by her husband (*The Burning Bed*); Theresa Saldana is stalked and stabbed by a maniac (*Victims for Victims*); the eldest son does not respond to permissive parenting and becomes a cocaine addict (*Toughlove*). Shortly after Revé Walsh realizes her son is missing, the comforting atmosphere of the shopping mall becomes a nightmarish maze; as in a horror film scenario, she runs through haunted corridors. The traumas portrayed in these films span the entire New Right agenda of the terrors posed to the nuclear family of the 1980s—everything from child abduction and murder to teenage cocaine use; indeed Kevin Phillips claims to have coined the term "New Right" in 1974 to describe populist-conservative groups more upset with the moral and cultural tone of liberalism than with its economic policies (1983, p. 47).

The victims/parents seek help through established institutions. In each case, the parents start out believing that justice will be achieved through these institutions. A crucial moment occurs when the outraged parent realizes it is otherwise. *Adam* sums it up it up when John Walsh says to the local police, "The FBI can locate your stolen truck but not your stolen child?" Similarly, Candy Lightner is shocked to discover early in the film that the man who killed her daughter will probably not even serve time, even though he is a repeat drunk driving offender. This function occupies a relatively brief moment in these films, but I include it because it is conceptually distinct from the next: none of the parents started out disillusioned with the system; their zealotry is a creation of circumstance. The implication is that any parent faced with a similar trauma could become a populist political activist.

The institutions are unable to help them and are shown to be totally inadequate. The critique of public institutions permeates and even defines this type of trauma drama. Todd Gitlin has made the point that both *Bitter Harvest* (1981) and *Lois Gibbs and the Love Canal* (1982)—early trauma dramas dealing with chemical dumping—are antistate not anticorporate (1983, p. 177). While I would agree that it is public sector institutions that these movies focus upon, I am not sure that Gitlin's implication to the converse—that these films are therefore pro-private enterprise—is really true either. The emphasis is more on the conflict between individual and institution, not on the superiority of multinational corporations. That is why, later in the decade, the attack may shift away from the legal system and toward other large institutions that are seen to be working against the interests of the individual family—the medical establishment, for example. This is also why a similar individual versus institution ideology could pervade other forms of eighties TV—talk shows and news magazines—in which the enemy frequently *was* corporate in nature. Although a number of bureaucracies that are scarcely bastions of liberalism come under attack (the FBI, the Veterans Administration, state legislatures), by far the most common villain in these films is a criminal justice system that places the rights of criminals above the rights of victims. As Theresa Saldana puts it in her autobiographical saga (and since it is "her story," we do not think that she is playing a part) after being told by a representative of the district attorney's Violent Crime Reimbursement Program that it might take a year to get the measly $10,000 worth of medical expenses to which she is entitled as a victim, "The man who tried to kill me is taken care of. He gets free room and board, free medical care."

The problem is not simply one of bureaucratic inefficiency, but rather of bureaucracies that have been rendered inefficient by the legal system itself. Clearly, there is a populist appeal based on economics alone; one of these films, *Many Happy Returns* (1986), even goes after the IRS, a bureaucracy unpopular with almost everyone. But it treats the situation comically, making the film most atypical. In the majority of cases, it is stated or implied that the bureaucratic failure is linked to the very concept of the liberal welfare state. These institutions are not only dysfunctional, they are hampered by laws that protect criminals and hamper victims in their pursuit of justice. In *The Burning Bed*, the desperate Francine repeatedly tries to get help as a victim of domestic violence. A social worker at the welfare office refuses her request, telling her, "You can't get welfare unless you separate from your husband," and "The courts will protect you" against him. After her divorce, when the county administration can't protect her, she realizes she is "totally on [her] own now." When she tells the county authorities that her ex-husband tried to kill her, they respond, "We'll have to let probation handle it, but come back and see us if there's any trouble." Finally, Aid to Families with Dependent Children tells her that the only thing they can do is take her welfare away.

This theme of the system's inability to help victims permeates the films from the beginning of the cycle. In *The Child Stealer* (1979), the law won't help a young mother get her children back from an ex-husband. Another 1979 film, *Mrs. R.'s Daughter,* shows a mother taking the law into her own hands to bring to trial her daughter's rapist. In the 1981 docudrama *Bitter Harvest,* a young farmer tries to find out what's killing his dairy herd, but his efforts are hampered by uncooperative state agricultural officials. *Broken Promise* (also 1981) shows a juvenile court services director battling odds to place siblings together despite bureaucratic opposition. Trauma dramas from 1984 include *With Intent to Kill,* in which a father avenges his daughter's death, pursuing the teen boy murderer who copped an insanity plea. *The Rape of Richard Beck* (1985) puts a grim twist on the rape versions of these trauma dramas; the hero is a macho police officer confronting the indifference of the system after he himself is raped. The same year, *Streets of Justice* has an auto worker turn vigilante after the killers of his wife and son get off on a legal technicality. In the 1986 *Vengeance: The Story of Tony Cimo,* a man again tires of waiting for the courts to act and has his parents' killer killed. In all of these examples, ordinary citizens come up against a legal system that actively works against the achievement of justice.

But it is not just the courts that are at fault. Other institutions come under fire as well. Two other public institutions—the military and the schools—are sometimes bad guys in trauma dramas. In *The Marva Collins Story* (1981), the heroic individual is a black school teacher who has to go outside the school system in order to educate poor black children. This may seem radical, yet the new and ultimately wildly successful institution she struggles to found is a classical academy for ghetto children that stresses universal humanistic values from the Western tradition—scarcely a bastion for ethnic pride and multiculturalism. Early in this docudrama, Collins appears at the Board of Education to argue over "recognition" of her school. She tells an uncooperative bureaucrat: "If I needed government handouts, I'd have to listen to them, and I don't want anyone telling me how to teach." At the end of the film we learn (not surprisingly) that President Reagan invited her to become secretary of education but that she declined, preferring to remain in the classroom.

Yet the frustration addressed by the populist discourse in these films is also aimed at capitalist and "private sector" bureaucracies. The medical establishment with its exorbitant costs and lack of concern for patients is the target of four 1987 films. In *Right to Die*, a woman with Lou Gehrig's disease has to fight both the legal and medical establishments (seen by the film as being in collusion) in order to achieve her goal of dying with dignity. In *Kids Like These*, the parents of a child born with Down's syndrome are discouraged from keeping their baby by the doctor that delivered him. In *Mercy or Murder*, the Robert Young character aids in the death of his wife who has Alzheimer's; in true populist fashion, the TV audience is asked to decide whether it was mercy or murder. Finally, in *Baby Girl Scott*, the parents of a severely disabled child have to fight the medical bureaucracy to let the infant die in the neonatal intensive care unit.

Even totally private sphere "institutions" are viewed as the source of social ills: in *Toughlove*, it is permissive child-rearing practices. Notably *not* a docudrama,[8] this film about a real-life organization nevertheless follows precisely the pattern of *M.A.D.D.*, *Adam*, and other films that criticize public institutions for allowing the idealized nuclear family to be destroyed and then letting the perpetrators get away with murder. Because its enemy lurks within the nuclear family itself, *Toughlove* seems especially symptomatic of the New Right bent the trauma drama took in the mid-1980s. Because it is a fictionalized film about a suburban high school assistant principal (the typical class status of center extremists) whose son has a drug problem, I did not at first identify *Toughlove* as one of the films that critiqued public institutions; rather I classified it as a domestic melodrama in which the problem was dealt with entirely inside the family. Yet the film's emphasis on the founding of the parental self-help group Toughlove was so extreme, its educational rhetoric so pronounced, that I began to see that this was the crucial film that linked the founding of new public institutions from the grass roots up to the crisis of the individual family that characterized the pure melodramas. When I identified the villain as yet another "public" institution—the permissive, liberal family of the 1960s and 1970s—I had the key to the position this film occupies within the group.

The film begins with a suburban rather than a pastoral idyll—the father and his two sons are about to purchase the older son's first car. What trauma could this innocuous event portend? The answer is given when the mother questions the father's indulgence of his son's whim. The trauma then unfolds, but not abruptly as when the perpetrator lies outside the family. As the nuclear family is doubled by a single mother with a wayward daughter, we come to realize that the problem is not drugs per se—although both teenagers have a drug problem—but rather the fact that these children are out of control. The solution lies not in understanding and psychological counseling—for as we will learn, these are the enemies of the nuclear family—but rather in the rebirth of the authoritarian family of pre-1960s America. This is the mission of the self-help organization that the reluctant parents attend, a mission stated point blank by the male facilitator at one of the parental discussion groups: "The Toughlove program was founded by a Pennsylvania couple—both professional counselors. Their incentive came one night when police surrounded their home with shot guns. . . . Their daughter was charged with holding up a cocaine dealer. Now, we're not talking about some back alley dope deal by poverty-stricken ghetto kids. This was suburban Pennsylvania. These are people like you and me with kids that are just plain out of control."

At this point the camera pans to pick up another discussion group where a woman speaks out against permissiveness. The rhetoric is fascinating: it's the kids that are tearing their families apart. The message is clear: psychology doesn't work; it doesn't matter how they got to be that way; parents have rights too. The repentant father renounces his professional training in "understanding" and eventually follows the most extreme advice of the organization by allowing his son to spend time in jail and locking him out of the house. "I don't care why you take drugs, Gary, but this is gonna stop right now. This isn't your house, it's our house and you have to live by our rules." This is where the self-help group—usually designed for psychological support—merges with the grass-roots political organization, for the goal of the Toughlove organization is the renunciation of psychology in favor of brute force. The fact that so many of the social ills of the decade penetrated to the very heart of the private sanctuary of the family meant that these "sociological" films dramatized the radical (but right-wing) politicization of the family crucial to the New Right agenda.

Many 1980s made-for-TV movies take the form of domestic melodramas in which the private ills are centered in the family; no public solution is offered in these films, but they are linked to the films under discussion by virtue of the social discontent they express. This list includes *Something about Amelia* (1984; incest), *Surviving* (1985; teen suicide), *Kate's Secret* (1986; bulimia), *Child's Cry* (1986; child abuse), *A Fight for Jenny* (1986; child custody), and numerous others. Not all films diagnose an authoritarian solution to the crisis of the family, but the fact that the loss of faith in institutions receives such widespread attention does give ammunition to groups seeking such solutions. That is to say, the critique of institutions feeds easily into the overall authoritarian populist atmosphere of the decade.

The victims take matters into their own hands. Both *M.A.D.D.* and *Adam* show parents of victims being reluctantly drawn into public life out of their sense of outrage at the flaws of the criminal justice system. As Candy Lightner tells a sympathetic attorney early in the film, "I'm not even registered to vote." These ordinary folks differ from real politicians in that they are not temperamentally suited for politics; they enter the political arena from the grass roots up. Yet it is precisely their close association with "the people" that endows them with nobility and enables them to succeed where the system has heretofore failed in protecting victims' rights.

Here is where the fanaticism of the parent/victim most comes into play, mirroring the oft-noted fanaticism of the New Right politics of the 1980s. As one observer noted, "For much of the 'new-right,' politics was analogous to a crusade which demanded the energy and conviction of a zealot" (Peele 1984, p. 9). Significantly, the motivation for the zealotry is often maternal love, the same force said to motivate the female New Right antiabortion activists. This motivation creates a contradictory position for the mothers portrayed in these films. In the deepest sense of New Right ideology, these are traditional women left behind by feminism. And yet, as in the case of many New Right ideologues, these mothers are the only people left in the culture who retain the moral righteousness necessary to the task. Therefore they (always reluctantly) take on a masculine role for the sake of their victimized children, or in some cases to help other victims of violent crimes. *Adam* reveals that they would rather a man do it when possible. In the movie, the Walshes meet for dinner with some mothers from the organization Child Find. The mothers plead with John Walsh to come to their aid: "We need your voice. You're a *father*. Up till now it's just been mothers of missing children—a father has to speak: *Be our voice, Mr. Walsh*" (italics mine).

In this way, the Walshes take on a traditionally gender-divided division of labor: Revé Walsh answers the phones at the Adam Walsh Outreach Center; John Walsh takes on the U.S. Congress. According to Nick Browne, "In the 1982–83 season, in contrast to the equal male/female viewing for theatrical films, the audience for made-for-TV movies was distinctly female" (1987, p. 594). He concludes that "women comprise, statistically and perhaps culturally, the most important part of the audience for those movie forms designed specifically for television." Perhaps these vigilante-mom made-for-TV films appealed to the same impulses as a right-wing feminism in support of the traditional family. In this sense, they could be considered "women's pictures" or even politicized melodramas.[9] They delineate those forms of political activism possible for ordinary women during the Reagan years.

They join a self-help group or form a grass-roots organization. Indeed many of the films are explicitly about the formation of organizations such as those from which *M.A.D.D.*, *Toughlove*, and *Victims for Victims* take their titles. Even films that do not otherwise follow this plot pattern often include a scene in which the victim of the film's trauma joins a self-help group. In *An Early Frost* and *Do You Remember Love?* (1985), this function seems almost unmotivated by the films' narratives; the group experience doesn't seem to help the victim or family, but nevertheless it seems crucial that it be included for the record. The hospital group therapy session for PWA's (Persons with AIDS) in which the "victim" in *An Early Frost* participates is so grim that he exits saying: "I don't want to be here. I don't belong here."

Even in *The Burning Bed*, which is about the victim's *inability* to get help from a variety of organizations, the nonstory materials (see below) are entirely about organizations that help victims of domestic violence. In *Adam* and *M.A.D.D.*, where what is founded is more a grass-roots political lobby than a self-help therapeutic group, the purpose of this function is clear: the charismatic individual will mobilize the people from the bottom up, succeeding where a host of bureaucracies have failed.

The new organization is better able to cope with the trauma, often having an impact on established institutions. Both *M.A.D.D.* and *Adam* resolve their plots in hard-won legislative victories: the former in the California State Assembly, the latter in the U.S. Congress. In the process of enacting legislation, the ordinary citizen is transformed into a charismatic politician. What this role involves is the ability to manipulate the media for the sake of the grass-roots organization or self-help group. *M.A.D.D.* deals explicitly with this issue (as does *Adam: His Song Continues*). Early in the film Candy is advised: "Organize. Form chapters of your organization. Start flexing your political muscles, get publicity." This advice echoes the strategy of New Right single-issue political campaigns in general and the antiabortion movement in particular, even though such a controversial issue gets displaced onto the "safer" one of drunk driving. Because she is "of the people" and because of her moral righteousness, Candy is allowed to behave in a most unfeminine manner. Indeed Candy's greatest victory occurs when she blackmails a lobbyist onto her side by threatening him with national media coverage of the vote against her M.A.D.D. bills. What Candy—the "innocent victim"—learns is how to put pressure on politicians and how to use the media to force them to act. In fact the media are the one public institution that escapes unscathed in these films.

Normality is restored (however inadequately). *Adam* both is and is not typical here. The final scene finds John Walsh back in the suburban kitchen with his wife and his mother, bathing his new baby (a sacred activity not to be interrupted by phone calls). But the call John Walsh receives is from the president of the United States, hardly a typical occurrence. *M.A.D.D.* ends with a similar summons to the White House; Candy's friend runs up to her at Cari's grave, waving an invitation from the president to attend the formation of a commission on drunk driving.

But the repeat showing of *Adam* goes even further. After John Walsh's mother tells him, "They say it's the White House," we cut to the real John Walsh, who intones: "It *was* the White House. I'm John Walsh." He introduces Revé and their two new children, who are "safer by the president's signing of the Missing Children's Assistance Act of 1984." "Mr. President, thank you from all our children." At this point Ronald Reagan appears on the screen to introduce the roll call of missing children that will end the broadcast. In case we didn't understand the populist message of the film itself, the president tells us, "Federal legislation is only the beginning." We need state and local efforts, as well, and "the rest is up to you."

The restoration of normality function is clearer in a domestic-issue-oriented film like *Toughlove*. It is Christmas day and the family is gathered together without, however, the out-of-control, prodigal, drug-addicted older son. When the boy finally makes an appearance, it is to return his signed contract and ask to enter a rehab program the next day. "I know what the rules are," he tells his tearful parents. Then, in an act that had my students gasping in horror, he washes $1,000 worth of cocaine down the suburban kitchen sink. The film ends with the father's final renunciation of the psychologistic tenets of liberal parenting ("It doesn't matter what the reason is") and with a tentative reconciliation between the bad boy and his normal younger brother. *Toughlove* well reflects the tenuousness with which normality is restored. The suggestion is that a new trauma could occur at any moment, that the stability of family life is fragile indeed. This tenuousness is reinforced by the real-life continuation of those films that are docudramas. We will read in *People* magazine that Theresa Saldana had to reappear in court to beg that her attacker not be released on parole. We will follow the real-life saga of John Walsh's rise to celebrity status and the threat this poses to the averageness of his family, the subject of the sequel: *Adam: His Song Continues*. As we see him hosting *America's Most Wanted*, we are reminded that there are still criminals out there that the FBI cannot catch without John Walsh's help and ours.

Although the films themselves do not *insist* on a reading in terms of the Reagan agenda, both the way the films were presented and the overall configuration of forces outside the films suggest that they would have been received as pro-Reagan critiques of liberal institutions and cries for the restoration of the old-fashioned American family. Moreover, the way these films were positioned in the overall flow of the nightly TV schedule and through media publicity helped to reinforce a conservative agenda. "Nonstory materials" may work against or serve to anchor the narratives ideologically. The printed titles at beginning and end, promos for the evening news and other postmovie events, and various public service announcements all interrupt the movie proper and influence audience readings of the films. Even a garden-variety TV commercial can have an impact on our reading of a socially relevant movie. In *God Bless the Child* (1988), a made-for-TV movie about a homeless woman who must give up her child, the squalid realism of the film's narrative was undercut by the many ads for food and other home-oriented items, suggesting that a mother who truly loved her child would have been able to provide her with, at the very least, some Proctor and Gamble products. The telefilm's commercials contrasted both with the film itself and with its promotional print advertising, which featured a stark black background with a Dorothea Lange–like photo of mother with child and the following copy in white lettering: "Watching this movie may make you uncomfortable. It reaches deep into your heart and conscience as it tells its story about two people who share our country but not its glories. Powerful. Disturbing. It may also be the most important movie you will see all year."

In addition, many local affiliates did followup segments on the late news linked to the topic discussed in the films. This followup was facilitated by the scheduling of the trauma dramas in the nine to eleven o'clock Sunday and Monday night slot that flows directly into the eleven o'clock news (these are also, respectively, "family" viewing and female viewing nights). Although it is possible that the news coverage could represent a more radical treatment of the topic covered in the movie, it is much more likely that the ongoing familial drama of the local news would attempt to reassure the local folks (although the local news is local only in details, not in format), whereas the one-shot trauma drama can afford to shake them up. In most cases, then, the coverage on the news suggests that the disturbing problem treated in the films is really resolvable. For example, after the 1987 film *Right to Die,* the NBC affiliate in Pittsburgh did a followup story on Lou Gehrig's disease that intercut scenes from the film with scenes of a man at a local hospital who suffered from the disease. But, unlike the character portrayed by Raquel Welch in the film, the local man is a religious Catholic who wishes to live, and the "expert doctor" interviewed on the news stresses what you *don't* lose with this disease—your mind, eyesight, hearing, bowel control—you are, he says, an "intact human being." This is exactly opposite to the message of the film but far more palatable to the largely Catholic local audience. Which version will they be likely to retain?

In a similar ideological anchoring of the message of a "public service drama," a story many years later on cable news used footage from *The Burning Bed* in a story about why the wives of alcoholics stay with their husbands. The news item greatly simplified the complex text of *The Burning Bed,* making it seem as if the film were simply about alcoholism. It is precisely the more complex films such as *The Burning Bed* (discussed below) that are susceptible to this kind of ideological centering by the nonstory materials. Even the ambiguous ending of the film is undercut by the printed titles at the end:

> The story of Francine Hughes introduces the problem of wife abuse but does not provide a solution. Killing her husband only added to the personal tragedy for Francine and her children. Domestic violence is serious and widespread. In recognition of this, many communities are setting up emergency hotlines and shelters for women and children.

This text comes at the end of a film that showed the inability of the victim to start or find a self-help group. In fact, the entire local broadcast of this film subverted the hopelessness of its narrative. During commercial breaks, numbers for local domestic violence hotlines were flashed on the screen. Just after a police officer tells Francine that he can't arrest her husband unless he is caught in the act, we see a pitch for a women's shelter, saying that the film is, "unfortunately, a true story," but implying that we can now solve the problem of domestic violence through strategies of self-help. In a promo for the eleven o'clock news, we see the female anchorperson watching the film with a group of battered wives and are promised "their reaction at eleven." Although the film suggests that wife abuse is a deep structural problem embedded in the contemporary nuclear family, the nonstory materials suggest easy solutions obtainable through the forming of self-help groups and grass-roots organizations in local communities.

And yet the sense of the fragility of the average American family implied at the end of every trauma drama has implications for the political meaning these films had in the context of Reaganism. Perhaps, like Reagan's own promises, these optimistic sagas of the rebirth of America through grass-roots populist zealotry were not quite believable. The tenuousness of even those films that play out the entire pattern suggests that the inflection of popular frustrations to the right was a massive ideological project even at the limited level of influencing readings of a few made-for-TV movies. As Kevin Phillips points out, as late as the mid-1970s pollsters disagreed as to whether the popular discontent around social issues they were recording would result in a move to the right or to the left (1983, p. 198). The fact that three of the most critically acclaimed trauma dramas of the mid-1980s—*The Burning Bed* (1984), *An Early Frost* (1985), and *Unnatural Causes* (1986)—are easily interpreted as left-wing or at least subversive inversions of the formula indicates the instability of the neoconservative reading of the films, an instability I would argue is related to but not identical with the instability of the Reaganite hegemony.[10]

Each of these films fails to complete all eight functions entailed in the general plot structure; it is the variations involved that allow them to be read against the grain of the more hegemonic films that contain all eight steps. *The Burning Bed* is especially ambiguous in this regard, perhaps because it deals with feminist/women's issues not amenable to placement on the usual left-right political spectrum. The failure to complete all eight functions is symptomatic of a larger ideological failure to inflect the film toward the New Right agenda. Although it is not obligatory that all eight functions appear in the usual order, for the most part in the more orthodox films, they do. The first hint of the unconventionality of *The Burning Bed* is that the scenes of normal family life do not commence until seven minutes into the film, in a flashback to the summer of 1963, when Francine Hughes fell in love with her prospective husband in a scene right out of a 1950s teenpic. Their courtship and early marriage follow in a similar idyllic vein. But all this has been prefaced by a flashback structure from a present time that finds Francine in jail for having set her husband on fire. The scenes of normative family life, then, are narrated from the perspective of its abysmal failure. In another inversion, we view the most traumatic event before we see any hint of the average family. I have already discussed the way in which this film stretches out functions 3 and 4: the victim (of wife abuse) seeks help from numerous organizations; the institutions are unable to help her and are shown to be totally inadequate. In fact this institutional failure is exaggerated in *The Burning Bed*, stretching out over a large middle portion of the telefilm. The trauma of abuse and the seeking of help are repeated several times in Francine's narration (the entire story is told from her point of view). This repetition makes the presence of function 5 (the victim takes matters into her own hands) and the consequent absence of function 6 (joining a self-help group or forming a grass-roots organization) all the more striking. For if Francine eventually does take matters into her own hands by killing her husband, it is precisely because she is unable to conceptualize any kind of help at all. A few minutes prior to the end of the film we see the burning incident again; at the verdict which follows, the meaning of the final shot of the film is ambiguous. The film

dissolves to a black-and-white freeze frame of her face and a slow zoom in to her eyes. The expression isn't easily readable. What are we to make of this ambiguity? Is *The Burning Bed* another right populist chronicle of a desperate act committed in a public void? Or is it a bold feminist gesture of a woman taking the law into her own hands when the nuclear family itself has failed as an institution? The film itself does not say.

In a similar way, the fictionalized drama about AIDS portrays a trauma so disruptive of the idealized nuclear family that the film is unable to complete the pattern.[11] *An Early Frost* begins easily enough with a romanticized version of a happy family's gathering at the parents' wedding anniversary; the only problem is that the handsome and successful son is a closeted gay man soon to be diagnosed with AIDS. Thus step 2, the introduction of the trauma, is also present. But the rest of the film takes the form of a family melodrama, meaning that functions 3 through 7 are omitted. Although, as described above, we do see a self-help group, it is the victim not the parents who attends, and the group does not lead to any kind of political action. The restoration of a (tenuous) family stability does resolve the narrative. Interestingly, part of the restoration of the family involves a sibling (in this case the pregnant sister) who embraces the prodigal son, just as it did in the ultimate right-wing version, *Toughlove*. The final credits even unwind over a family portrait.

Why are crucial steps omitted from this film? Clearly, because the threat that the son's gayness poses to the theme of the restoration of family life is too great to be portrayed on TV; it has yet to be portrayed in any made-for-TV movie. Ironically and tragically, the number of case studies available for docudramas about AIDS increases daily. The eight-step sequence of plot functions would adapt easily to this real-life material: a young man stricken with AIDS unites with his lover to join ACT UP; in the process the U.S. government's attitude toward AIDS research is completely changed; a cure for the disease is found as the lovers embrace under the final credits. Interestingly, a version of this plot did appear as a dream sequence in the 1990 film *Longtime Companion*; similar texts (such as Larry Kramer's play *The Normal Heart)* have taken on the anti-institutional parts of the story.[12] But the subject matter tests the limits of the liberal side of the spectrum, just as on the other side of the spectrum, the trauma drama has not been able to accommodate the antiabortion movement or religious fundamentalism (except in the cases of those televangelists who have already disgraced themselves publicly). Thus I agree to some extent with critics who have argued that made-for-TV movies pull issues back to the center, but I disagree that, because of this, they are not radical forces (see Gitlin 1983, p. 157; Schulze 1990). I believe these critics have not examined the films in the context of the overall Reaganite political and cultural formation. In an era of "center extremism," centrist issues can be extreme cases.

It is important to remember that even those films that go through the entire eight-step sequence may have a subversive agenda. For

Friendly Fire, the fact that the mother's crusade was to end the Vietnam War allowed that film to show the impact Peg Mullen had on the side of a liberal cause. But of course that liberal cause was no longer controversial at the time the film was made, and it was just as easy for another Vietnam War trauma drama to inflect the eight-part structure to the conservative side, as did the 1988 *To Heal a Nation*, which detailed a charismatic and fanatical individual's fight to build the Vietnam Veterans Memorial. Now, however, the trauma is that the veterans are forgotten as war heroes, and the solution lies in memorializing those who died in Vietnam. The memorial itself becomes the grass-roots organization that reconstructs the Vietnam War for the eighties.

The fact that the war was long over, however, did not dull the radical edge of the John Sayles–scripted *Unnatural Causes* (1986), which dealt with the still current issue of the continuing harm done to veterans by the chemical Agent Orange used in Vietnam. No doubt to counter its liberalism, the film contains lengthy disclaimers at the beginning and end. When printed titles say that "*one* woman, Maude de Victor, worked with Chicago veterans and brought their grievances to public awareness" (emphasis mine), the intent may not be to stress Maude's charismatic individualism but rather to minimize the scope of a problem still under litigation. *Unnatural Causes* follows the basic pattern of the right-wing films but with significant variations. The normal, happy American family is seen under the credits as John Ritter plays with his kids, but we soon learn that he is divorced. When, at the usual early moment in the film, he is given the diagnosis of cancer and suspects that Agent Orange is at fault, the trauma drama would seem to be unfolding along its typical trajectory. But a significant variation occurs when the victim himself and a black woman not romantically involved with him become the fanatics seeking to establish the truth. Although only two individuals are represented in detail, collectivity is implied to a greater extent than is usual. Maude de Victor does seek help from an established institution—her employer, the Veterans Administration—and the institution does prove ineffective. But the critique of bureaucracy is more one of the Watergate than the Reagan era, for the Veterans Administration proves to be involved in a cover-up that threatens Maude's own livelihood. Ultimately, she must take her case to the media—just as Candy Lightner did—but the media event takes the form of an exposé on *60 Minutes*.[13] The critique of the Veterans Administration is a serious one, reinforced by the kind of bittersweet plot resolution that characterized *Friendly Fire*. Maude returns to work after her appearance on *60 Minutes* only to learn that her comrade and fellow crusader has died overnight. Through her tears, she begins to take the hundreds of phone calls that pour in in response to the segment. In fact the use of phone calls and letters is one of the chief methods by which collectivity is implied in these individualized narratives. Large chunks of the narrative of *Friendly Fire* are communicated through the reading of letters to the Mullens from veterans and their families. Revé Walsh is motivated to form the Adam Walsh Outreach Center when, after returning home from an attempt to recover from their son's death, she and John find their entire garage filled with letters from outraged parents. Yet in *Unnatural Causes* collectivity is represented as the culmination of the film's narrative trajectory—the impact of Maude's efforts themselves yield a response of collective outrage and protest. We do not see Maude de Victor going on to transform establishment institutions into instruments of populist collectivity. In fact, the printed titles at the end of the film inform us that she was subsequently fired from the Veterans Administration in a "labor dispute." The film does not resolve in the rebirth of America through right-wing individualist populist activity. It retains its leftist critical edge, while remaining fully within the category of the institutional trauma drama I have been describing.

It's important to remember that populism is not in itself a right-wing strategy;[14] it has been and could again be an instrument for collective action and even socialism. In his study of the agrarian revolt of the late nineteenth century, Lawrence Goodwyn (1978, pp. 35) repeatedly stresses that populism "was not an individual trait but a collective one, surfacing as the shared hope of millions organized . . . into its cooperative crusade" (1978, p. 35). Goodwyn also repeatedly stresses the difficulty of accomplishing a true democratic revolution in a nation structured by hierarchy to a greater extent than we like to admit. Both the analysis and the warning are applicable to the 1980s and to the case at hand.

For populism was to arise again in the presidential campaign of 1992. This time the fact that "center extremism" emerged in both the Perot and Clinton campaigns in itself demonstrates the volatility of populism through the eighties and into the nineties. Indeed Clinton's own story might form the subject of a made-for-TV movie. To wit: a young boy raised by his widowed mother attends Oxford, becomes governor of Arkansas, and against tremendous odds galvanizes single mothers, gays, and other disenfranchised groups in order to become president of the United States. If Bush was able to capitalize on the elitism of the Reagan formation, he was not able to latch onto its populism. Clinton played Reagan's populism against Bush in the savviest media campaign ever waged. Perhaps he learned a few things from the trauma dramas of the 1980s.

Notes

1 Alternative terms used to describe what I am calling the trauma drama. See Laurie Schulze 1990, p. 352.

2 From temperance novels to the muckraking tradition to Hollywood social problem films to recent drama documentary films such as *Silkwood* (1983). Gary Edgerton traces the contemporary problem orientation of the made-for-TV movie back to the 1950s live anthology series (1985). He also cites the increasing "relevancy" of the made-for-TV movie during the late 1970s and into the 1980s.

3 A term coined by Seymour Lipset to describe the frustrated middle classes of the Reagan coalition. Consisting of small businessmen, farmers, artisans, white-collar workers, and some professional elements, this "center" is suspicious of big business, big labor, and big government. Discussed in Phillips 1983, pp. 195–197.

4 This trend reached its apotheosis with 1994's *The Joan and Melissa Rivers Story,* in which the title characters reenacted the suicide of Edgar Rosenberg and its aftermath. The ghoulish voyeurism of this attempt to take the term "reenactment" to a new level should not be allowed to obscure its aesthetic significance.

5 Theresa Saldana's career as a professional victim continued when she hosted Lifetimes' *Confessions of Crime* in the summer of 1991—except that this time the crimes were narrated from the criminal's point of view.

6 The films are so similar that it is surprising to find no overlap between their production personnel; however both aired on NBC.

7 The term "function" is adapted from Vladimir Propp (1968). My use of it resembles more the kind of "Proppian analysis" employed by Will Wright (1975) and Janice Radway (1984) than it does the original analysis of Russian folktales. Both Wright and Radway use this type of structural narrative analysis to reveal in skeletal form the ideological impetus of a group of popular culture narrative texts that share a common structure. Variations as well as similarities are crucial.

8 Although the Toughlove organization had made the news when ABC's *Nightline* had its cameras in a home where a fifteen-year-old boy was ordered out after refusing to sign a contract to go into drug rehabilitation. According to *TV Guide,* "He carried a shopping bag of clothing as he left, glancing back over his shoulder at the strange sight of a TV camera and his parents huddled together by a window to record his departure" (1985, p. 11).

9 Similar to liberal feminist programs of the 1980s (see next chapter), these made-for-TV women's films frequently found their way to the 4:00 P.M. Lifetime movie slot during the 1990s.

10 Kevin Phillips's book stressed this instability from the beginning, saying that the coalition empowered in 1980 is very unstable (1983, p. xv). Subsequent developments bore this out.

11 My analysis of *An Early Frost* is indebted to an unpublished paper written by Steve Wurtzler at the University of Iowa (1988).

12 When it finally came to TV via HBO in September 1993, the long-awaited teleren-

dering of Randy Shilts's *And the Band Played On* looked remarkably like a made-for-TV movie. Centering on a crusading (and presumably heterosexual) male researcher at the CDC, the film streamlined Shilts's narrative to focus on the hero's struggles against two institutions: the governmental medical research bureaucracy and the gay establishment in San Francisco. This rendering gave the audience alternate target institutions on which to focus blame. Unlike in the Reaganite trauma dramas, the individual was not able to triumph over bureaucracy, nor could he reenergize institutions from the grass roots up. And when Ronald Reagan appears in the film, it is not as final summit. It would seem that AIDS remains outside the scope of resolvable dilemmas.

13 Three 1981 trauma dramas are based on stories first reported on *60 Minutes*. *The Marva Collins Story* was based on a 1979 segment about a Chicago schoolteacher who worked outside the system to help black children. *Thornwell* and *A Matter of Life and Death* were based on *60 Minutes* stories from 1978 and 1979. The former involved an anti–U.S. Army exposé; the latter was about a nurse who defied the hospital bureaucracy to start an unconventional program for terminally ill patients. The fact that the subject matter for these telefilms should be mediated through coverage on a news magazine should not really surprise us. The immensely popular *60 Minutes* has maintained the muckraking tradition from the post-Watergate era through the Reagan era with no signs of diminishing popularity. It retains a close relationship to the films under discussion, and its survival in both liberal and conservative times can be explained in similar ways.

14 Indeed in the nineties, the pendulum appears to be swinging back, especially when the trauma concerns women's issues. *Shattered Trust*, broadcast on NBC on 27 September 1993, concerned a woman lawyer's battle to change the incest law. The film seems remarkable in that it completes all eight functions, including the successful changing of the law in the California state legislature. The conclusion of the film, during which the new law passes, is so reminiscent of *M.A.D.D.* (a full ten years later) that it is uncanny. Yet the issue—incest—is treated as a feminist one; although victims' rights are emphasized, they are rights that exist at the expense of white male privilege, and the film explicitly states that the problem could not be resolved through the courts because there are too many Reagan-appointed right-wing judges.

2

The Yuppie Spectator

In a footnote to his own brief but suggestive comments on the historical consumers of postmodern art, Fredric Jameson alludes to the "meager analytical literature" on "yuppies" (1991, p. 430). Whether or not you agree with him depends on what you mean by "analytical." For while there is little scholarly literature on yuppies and especially not much Marxist analysis of yuppies, there was a great deal written about them by journalists (especially in 1984, dubbed the "year of the yuppie" by *Newsweek*) and a great deal of research on the subject by demographers of both the political science and the marketing variety. In addition, discussions of the "professional-managerial" class and of "baby boomers" preceded the coining of the term "yuppie" in 1983.

According to *Newsweek* (1984a, p. 14), the first usage of the term in print was by *Chicago Tribune* columnist Bob Greene. In an article entitled "Jerry Rubin's New Business Is Business," Greene wrote, "While he and Abbie Hoffman once led the Yippies—the Youth International Party—one social commentator has ventured that Rubin is now attempting to become the leader of the Yuppies—Young Urban Professionals" (1983).[1] The quotation stresses the continuity of the baby boom generation from a period of social protest to a period of concentration on corporate upward mobility in the 1980s. Another dimension of the term is brought out in the *Oxford English Dictionary*, which defines "yuppie" as "a *jocular* term for a member of a socio-economic group comprising young professional people working in cities" (emphasis mine). The OED traces the usage to the satiric 1984 *Yuppie Handbook*. Of the numerous citations given under the terms "yuppie," "yuppiedom," "yuppieism," and "yuppification," many are derogatory. For example: "We have got to break this Yuppie image." "What a curve, that, from hippiedom to yuppiedom." "Occasionally they are overcome by the instinct to perpetuate Yuppiedom with their little Yuppies." "I played second base for Our Lady of the Assumption.... I don't deal in yuppieisms." The note of hostility differentiates the term "yuppie" from the more neutral term "baby boomer" and from the Marxian "professional-managerial class" (PMC). Yuppies were also called the new class of neoconservatives or neoliberals in that they combined fiscal conservatism and relatively liberal social values, which distinguished them from Right populism.

Writing in 1988, Hendrik Hertzberg argued that "yuppiedom is essentially a phenomenon of the Ronald Reagan era, inextricably tied to the values, follies, and peculiar conditions thereof. . . . What we are dealing with . . . is something that began as a demographic category with cultural overtones and ended up as a moral category. *Yuppie* is now understood almost universally as a term of abuse" (p. 101). Although the term continues to be used, many believe the moment of the yuppie came to a close with the stock market crash of 19 October 1987, about the same time as the waning of the *Dynasty* craze and six days after the third episode of *thirtysomething* (both discussed below).

With all its negative connotations and elitist appeal, yuppiedom would not seem to be sufficiently mass-market for TV. Why then, in 1987, was an article in *Rolling Stone* entitled "Yuppievision" conceptualizing *thirtysomething* and *A Year in the Life* as programs by, for, and about yuppies (Minsky 1987)? In fact, in order to talk about the media construction of what was already a media construction, a few distinctions need to be made. We need to distinguish among *the yuppie audience* (a cultural category that affects demographics and thus a TV-industrial category); *yuppie representations* (signifiers of yuppies and yuppie culture in programs and ads whether direct [e.g., restaurants] or mediated [e.g., disillusioned cops, doctors, lawyers]), and *the yuppie spectator* (a construct of the analyst, i.e., anyone who can even momentarily be placed in a yuppie subject position).

The Yuppie Audience

A surprising proportion of the literature on yuppies consists of debates over how many there are. Both radicals debating the concept of the "professional-managerial class" and marketers debating the concept of the "baby boom generation" were interested in the same questions: how many are there? and what kind of influence do they have? Of course their motivations for counting differed: the Marxists wanted to mobilize this class or class fragment for radicalism; the marketers wanted to see if they constituted a unified market for products. Both the ideological and the economic components are important to an analysis of yuppies and TV.

The professional-managerial class was a concept developed by Barbara and John Ehrenreich in the late 1970s to explain why the working classes in the United States weren't radical like the intelligentsia. The Ehrenreichs argued that a new "middle class" category of workers must be considered for Marxist analysis; they saw this professional-managerial group as a "distinct class in monopoly capitalist society," one that had an "objectively antagonistic relationship" to the working class. They went on to define this PMC as "consisting of salaried mental workers who do not own the means of production and whose major function in the social division of labor may be described broadly as the reproduction of capitalist culture and capitalist class relations." The Ehrenreichs consider this group to be a class because they believe "a class is characterized by a coherent social and cultural existence; members of a class share a common life style, educational background, kinship networks, consumption patterns, work habits, beliefs." Much of the debate over the term "PMC" consisted of questioning their definition of "class" (Ehrenreich and Ehrenreich 1979, pp. 11-12).

What links the PMC debate to the coming of the term yuppie in 1984 is the way in which, while appearing to remain within a Marxian/socialist analysis, this intermediate class gets redefined in terms of *lifestyle* (an eighties term if there ever was one) rather than in terms of any objective relationship to the means of production. Fred Pfeil picks up the term "PMC" in his 1985 discussion (published in Pfeil, 1990) of postmodernism as the culture of the professional-managerial class. Attempting to resist global, totalizing definitions of postmodernism, Pfeil instead wants to define it "not as the inevitable extrusion of an entire mode of production but as a cultural-aesthetic set of pleasures and practices created by and for a particular social group at a determinate moment in its collective history. . . . Postmodernism is preeminently the expressive form of the social and material life-experience of my own generation and class, respectively designated as the 'baby boom' and the 'professional-managerial class'" (1990, pp. 97–125; quote on p. 105). Although neither Pfeil nor the Ehrenreichs use the term "yuppie" to define the class or generation whose culture and politics they are trying to understand, it is clear that the emphasis on lifestyle, work habits, educational background, consumption patterns, expressive forms, and so forth, suggests the term "yuppie"; it is not surprising that Fredric Jameson would include it in the context of his discussion of postmodernism as the culture of the PMC/yuppie class fraction:

For one can also plausibly assert that "postmodernism" in the more limited sense of an ethos and a "life-style" (truly a contemptible expression, that) is the expression of the "consciousness" of a whole new class fraction that largely transcends the limits of the groups enumerated above. This larger and more abstract category has variously been labeled as a new petit bourgeoisie, a professional-managerial class, or more succinctly as "the yuppies" (each of these expressions smuggling in a little surplus of concrete social representation along with itself). . . . This identification of the class content of postmodern culture does not at all imply that yuppies have become something like a new ruling class, merely that their cultural practices and values, their local ideologies, have articulated a useful dominant ideological and cultural paradigm for this stage of capital. It is indeed often the case that cultural forms prevalent in a particular period are not furnished by the principal agents of the social formation in question (businessmen who no doubt have something better to do with their time or are driven by psychological and ideological motive forces of a different type). What is essential is that the cultural ideology in question articulate the world in the most useful way functionally, or in ways that can be functionally reappropriated. Why a certain class fraction should provide these ideological articulations is a historical question as intriguing as the question of the sudden dominance of a particular writer or a particular style. There can surely be no model or formula given in advance for these historical transactions; just as surely, however, we have not yet worked this out for what we now call postmodernism. (Jameson 1991, p. 98)

The fact that leftists such as the Ehrenreichs, Pfeil, and Jameson could appropriate PMC culture for the left/academic intelligentsia indicates a link between this social group and the higher-income, capitalist-oriented yuppies. That link could be described as the sharing of "postmodern" culture despite differences in income and politics. In a sense, during the 1980s Marxist academics were yuppies who couldn't afford BMWs. They shared much of the artistic culture, the physical fitness boom, the career drive, the food culture. They shared the generational trajectory from counterculture to fanatical careerism. Although Pfeil, for instance, is willing to describe himself as a baby boomer, he is not willing (at least in the article) to describe himself as a "yuppie." But neither is anyone else. According to an editor's note in *American Demographics*, "The funny thing is, no one has ever found a yuppie. Not even the people who look and sound remarkably like yuppies will admit to being yuppies. . . . The yuppie is a mythical demographic beast, the public's attempt to put a human face on the nation's economic problems" (Russell 1988, p. 2).

Since the yuppie is a construct, not a thing, it is possible for groups deeply scornful of the-other-as-yuppie to deny the term applies to them. And yet postmodern culture, a more favorable term to some on the left, is also, at least in part, yuppie culture: both Fred Pfeil (1990, p. 108) and *The Yuppie Handbook* (Piesman and Hartley 1984, p. 68) invoke Laurie Anderson and Philip Glass as the high end of the cultural spectrum.

The concept of *generation* is crucial to Pfeil's notion of the class that consumes postmodern culture. Curiously, a similar debate permeates the marketing literature on the baby boomers. "What will the Superclass baby boomers buy?" asked one researcher in 1980. "The real question is whether tastes and preferences are based in certain ages or in certain generations" (Jones 1980, p. 189). The burning question for marketers about the "superclass" of the baby boom—soon to become the yuppies—was whether many of the products they consumed could be considered youth products or baby boom products. This is actually the same question that Fred Pfeil asks when he wonders if what we now call postmodern culture is really a generational culture of the baby boom. For those of us marketing ideas about postmodernism this is the crucial question because, we too will need to keep up with the trends. Perhaps Laurie Anderson is the arugula of performance art. At any rate, an obsession with yuppie counting infected both Marxists and marketers during the 1980s. Because they believed the PMC to be the class from which social change would emanate, the socialists were interested in amassing the largest possible numbers for the PMC or baby boom. They did not try to count "yuppies" specifically. According to the Ehrenreichs, the PMC includes something like fifty million people. Their "crude estimate" of the class composition of U.S. society allots 65 to 70 percent to the working class, 8 to 10 percent to the old middle class, 20 to 25 percent to the PMC, and 1 to 2 percent to the ruling class (1979, p. 14). According to Pfeil's even more optimistic figures, the overwhelming majority of U.S. citizens who in 1980 were between twenty-five and thirty-five years of age were members of the PMC, at least occupationally (1990, p. 98).

More mainstream sources, however, wanted to count yuppies specifically and to downplay their significance, because part of creating the yuppie image consisted of positing a large group of baby boomers who were *not* yuppies and to whom the authors thus belonged. Thus for Delli Carpini and Sigelman yuppies comprise only 2.4 percent of the 1972 to 1985 GSS respondent pool, only 5 percent of those less than forty years of age, only 9 percent of the urbanites, and only 16 percent of the professionals. "In short, yuppies are an extremely small proportion of both the population as a whole and of the relevant subpopulations" (1986, p. 515). The *Newsweek* cover story cites the California think tank SRI International, which, using as a working definition an income of $40,000 or more from a professional or management job, concluded that there were 4 million Americans between ages twenty-five and thirty-nine who fit that description and only about 1.2 million of those actually lived in a city. *Newsweek* succinctly concluded, "This is the *creme fraiche* of Yuppies, an elite so small that you could fit them all, four to a car, in all the BMW's in America" (1984, p. 16). Similarly, *American Demographics* found only 4.2 million baby boomers (a minuscule 5 percent) to qualify as yuppies in 1985. The 2.2 million households headed by yuppies represented only 6 percent of the households headed by baby boomers; fully 72 percent of yuppie households were headed by married couples, compared with 58 percent of all baby boom households. Yet less then 8 percent of baby boom married couples fell into the yuppie category: "Although yuppies are the most visible baby boomers, the downscale side of the boom is much larger. Because people are likely to buy products and services that make them feel more upscale than they are, the yuppie image has greater influence than the numbers suggest" (*American Demographics* 1985, p. 29).

Do yuppies matter? This is the question political scientists Michael Delli Carpini and Lee Sigelman want to answer through statistical analysis. They point out that most definitions of yuppies employ both demographic and lifestyle criteria and thus confuse the presumed consequences of yuppiedom with the phenomenon itself. As we have seen, the authors find that those meeting the literal definition of yuppie—young and urban and professional—are quite rare. After exhaustive statistical analysis, they conclude: "We have uncovered virtually no evidence that would support the yuppie class thesis, the notion that a synergism among the component elements of yuppiedom makes yuppies somehow *sui generis* politically. The generally liberal stands of yuppies are explainable without reference to any yuppie class or new class notion. . . . For "yuppie" to be a useful construct in understanding contemporary politics, it must be defined with precision [yet] as the definition of yuppies becomes less amorphous, the political significance of yuppie status becomes more ephemeral" (1986, p. 516).

Yet it was precisely the amorphous definition of yuppiedom as a state of mind or lifestyle that made it suitable for media image construction if not for building a political voting bloc or movement. Because of the appeal of the yuppie image to what was actually a sizable downwardly mobile generation,[2] yuppie culture could be mobilized for media images. Like so many phenomena of the eighties—including Ronald Reagan himself—the yuppie was a nonexistent phantom figure whose effect as image was nevertheless real.

Yuppie Representations on TV

The yuppie image was indelibly fixed by two media events of 1984— the *Newsweek* cover story "The Year of the Yuppie" and *The Yuppie Handbook*. These publications developed the yuppie stereotype for the broader population. But yuppie culture had developed earlier. The passage from hippiedom to yuppiedom is commemorated in the 1983 film *The Big Chill.*[3] *Metropolitan Home* magazine, the bible of urban gentrification, postmodern design, and California cuisine began publication in 1981, the same year it informed us that "pink is the new beige." Yuppie culture and writing about it was always tongue-in-cheek, to a greater or lesser degree. The *Newsweek* issue and the *Handbook* were no exceptions. The *Newsweek* cover features Doonesbury cartoon his-and-hers yuppies, complete with briefcase, running shoes, and business suits. Inside, however, we got to see the real thing—a full page photograph of two New York yuppies, dressed for work and sport. These "real" images are uncanny because they exactly duplicate the cartoon figures on the cover of *The Yuppie Handbook*, complete with pin stripe suits, Burberry trench coat, squash racket, and gourmet shopping bag filled with fresh pasta. Which came first, the reality or the cartoon? Or are we in the situation Jean Baudrillard describes when he writes: "The very definition of the real becomes: that of which it is possible to give an equivalent reproduction. . . . The real is not only what can be reproduced, but that which is always already reproduced" (1983, p. 146)?

The yuppies interviewed in the story say things like "I'm totally infatuated with the world of real estate" and "without children I would be comfortable with $200,000 a year." The authorial voice gives itself away when it writes, "Even secular Yuppies frequently describe a kind of Epiphany, a sudden realization that poverty might never live up to its romantic promise" (*Newsweek*, 1984a, p. 19). *The Yuppie Handbook* portrays two humorless latter-day preppies, Michael and Jennifer, as they go about embodying the yuppie lifestyle: eating out, buying expensive

kitchen equipment, furnishing their gentrified condos according to floor plans suggested in the manual, going to the gym, and climbing the corporate fast track (Piesman and Hartley 1984).

Although these documents (especially the *Handbook*) give the impression that yuppies were deadly serious about their consumerism and self-interest, in fact, it is arguable that the whole tone of yuppie culture was self-mocking. If this is true, then *The Yuppie Handbook* gives a false impression of the source of the humor—it's not *us* making fun of those yuppies but always *us* making fun of ourselves at the same time as we take ourselves utterly seriously. Even the intimidating statistical analysis by two political scientists in *Public Opinion Quarterly* has a bizarre ring to it: as they critique the definition of the yuppie given in the satiric *Yuppie Handbook*, a footnote informs us, "The cutoff of 39 years old is somewhat arbitrary, and has occasioned much bitterness on the part of one of the co-authors" (Delli Carpini and Sigelman 1986, p. 504). The self-distancing is both generational and historical— the former flower children laughing at their own materialism, the former war protesters laughing at their neoconservatism. That's why *Metropolitan Home* always employs the royal "we" as in "a magazine for the way *we* wanted to live"—except that the "we" isn't royal, it's talking about our generation, to paraphrase the song. This double-voiced quality appears again and again during the 1980s—in yuppie self-irony, in camp attitudes toward *Dynasty*, in the complicitous critique of postmodern art. It signals an ultimate admission that the fantastic Reaganite world we are caught up in has something amiss at its core. The unselfconscious yuppie was truly a media myth created by yuppie journalists.

Unsuccessful Yuppie-Representation Shows: *Jack and Mike, Heartbeat*

What, then, were the elements of this mythical yuppie culture that could be adapted to media and specifically to television representations?

1. Career obsessiveness, especially for women. But unlike 1950s corporate culture, work for baby boomers has to be personally meaningful.
2. A busy life. Yuppies are always busy, so that just as work becomes personal, personal life becomes work. *The Yuppie Handbook* brings this out.
3. Emphasis on the two-career childless couple; later in the decade an emphasis on children.
4. Materialism expressed in home decoration, food, and restaurant culture.
5. Physical fitness as work.
6. Equality for women; sensitivity for men.

All of these "lifestyle" elements of yuppie culture were adapted to certain TV series in the mid- to late eighties (see appendix B). The shows were clustered at the end of the decade, due to the penetration of yuppie culture into the mainstream and industrial factors such as the introduction of the people meter, which made yuppie counting more precise. The prime-time schedule staked out certain time slots as "yuppie" slots. For the fall 1986 season on ABC it was *Moonlighting* at 9:00, *Jack and Mike* at 10:00; for 1987 it was still *Moonlighting* at 9:00 with *thirtysomething* filling the yuppie slot at 10:00. Similarly, Thursday at 10:00 on NBC was first occupied by *Hill Street Blues*, later by *L.A. Law*. But the term "yuppie show" is imprecise. After laboriously elaborating yuppie culture, it seems to me that only a few of these programs directly represented the yuppie lifestyle for TV. Other shows that appealed to yuppie audiences did not necessarily represent yuppie culture. *Dallas* and *Dynasty*, for instance, portrayed the ruling class. *Moonlighting* traded on nostalgia for the Hollywood hardboiled tradition, although its commercials contained numerous representations of yuppie culture.

Two programs, however, captured the "look" of yuppie culture; neither of them succeeded in the ratings. *Jack and Mike* (fall 1986) and *Heartbeat* (spring 1988) were created by, produced by, or written by journalist and author Sara Davidson, a noted chronicler of the sixties generation of women who had become a cutting-edge commentator on yuppie culture. The transition from her first to her second book is conveyed by their titles: *Loose Change: Three Women of the Sixties* (1977) and *Real Property* (1980). Although it was hyped to become a hit show, *Jack and Mike* could not make it in the Neilsens.

Could its failure have been caused in part by a too-direct representation of the yuppie lifestyle? Jackie and Mike are young, urban, and professional to a fault. She has personally meaningful work as a newspaper columnist. He runs numerous yuppie restaurants, each replicating a different style of yuppie dining, for example, an Ed de Bevics–style diner and a restaurant serving *nouvelle cuisine*. They are work-obsessed—she writes a column called "No Time for Sex," which becomes a running joke in the pilot episode. Jackie and Mike appear to reproduce the comic parody of overscheduling enjoyed by our fictional yuppies in the *Handbook*. Even so, they are far more developed as characters than the "real life" yuppies interviewed in the *Newsweek* cover story. They live in a Chicago gentrified brownstone in a condo that could occupy an editorial spread in *Metropolitan Home*. Their lamps are the de rigueur halogen torchieres. Their kitchen, prominently displayed on the screen, contains shelves upon shelves of expensive cookware, built-in ovens, and the stainless steel Sub-Zero refrigerators then popular only in the most advanced yuppie homes. In one scene, the camera lingers for a close-up of their espresso/cappuccino maker.

Jackie and Mike's bathroom also comes in for prominent visual display. Upon arising in the morning, Jackie and Mike stagger into their immense spa, complete with his-and-hers sinks, black and white tile, and exercise equipment.

Although *Heartbeat* is more an ensemble cast than a solo focus on the double-income, no-kids, two-career couple, it nevertheless retains the visual emphasis on yuppie postmodern design features; the sets are displayed prominently in each episode, just as the lavish ruling class sets were displayed on *Dynasty*. Apparently a deep dedication to providing feminist gynecological services to women is more profitable than one might have expected, for the Women's Medical Arts building is a marvel of architectural design. The open plan has the cut-out walls and glass block interior windows, not to mention the grayed-out pastel palette favored by postmodern interior decorators. One would imagine it to be a far cry from the buildings where feminist health services are actually provided; nevertheless, the set was based on the offices of Sara Davidson's own OB/GYN in Los Angeles.

Although *Jack and Mike* and *Heartbeat* emphasized visual representations of the yuppie lifestyle, they combined these with the old heroic archetypes of the TV investigative and medical genres, respectively. Yuppiedom thus became a set of visual codes that could be reproduced across media—whether narrative or pictorial. According to Landon Jones, members of the baby boom superclass do not "see a dichotomy between private and social values and have no intention of denying their 'real selves' on the job. In their minds, self-fulfillment and successful careers should not be incompatible. The purpose of a job, they argue, is not to satisfy their material needs but to satisfy their emotional needs.... Their work must be meaningful and provide an outlet for self-expression. In a way, they want to be students again" (1980, p. 284). The emphasis on career leads me to classify shows such as *Cagney and Lacey* and *Kay O'Brien* as yuppie shows, even though they do not otherwise convey yuppie culture. Career is also the area in which yuppie cultural values overlap with those of (bourgeois) media feminism in both programming and advertising. Yuppie programs stress the meaningfulness of work; arguably the work-family concept from *The Mary Tyler Moore Show* on was an outgrowth of baby boom values.

The fact that so many of the yuppie shows considered failures by the networks wound up on the Lifetime Cabletelevision Network (especially since most of them did not have enough episodes for regular syndication) points to a nonnetwork narrowcasting strategy that was not yet a major force in the 1980s. Lifetime thinks of itself as a cable service for "delivering" not babies but their baby boomer mothers to advertisers. Founded in the year of the yuppie (1984), the Lifetime Cabletelevision Network had by 1988 solidified its position as the top cable network for reaching a female audience. It reaches a small but select audience, as did the more authentic yuppie cultural media (e.g., *Metropolitan Home* and *New York* magazines, restaurants, Banana Republic retail shops), and assures its owners—Capital Cities/ABC, Hearst Corp., and, during the 1980s, Viacom International—of a continued stake in the market as the network shares decline. Its president has stated: "Magazines and radio went from mass-market vehicles to segmentation. TV is going through the same transformation. We're at an age when cable is moving toward personalization. The bulk of what we do is demographically pure. We want to reach upscale working women without diluting the audience. To me, the attractiveness we've provided advertisers in the advent of people meters is a predictable demographic profile. It's a safety net to advertisers" (*Advertising Age* 1988, p. S-22).

The language used here is that of chemistry but also that of fascism. James Fennimore, president of Cable Networks, Inc., makes it even clearer. "We've already deleted the old, poor and underemployed from the viewing mix," he told *Variety*. Fennimore's article explains that while cable executives may only be able to deliver one thousand homes, they deliver a "quality" one thousand homes (1989, p. 38). The metaphor of racial purity explains why Lifetime found desirable shows that had flopped on the networks: *Kay O'Brien, Jack and Mike, Heartbeat, Molly Dodd,* and the always marginal *Cagney and Lacey.* Repackaged, these programs that contained the most cutting-edge representations of bourgeois feminism to appear on the networks during the early to mid-1980s could be sold to a "select" audience as programs for "working women," thereby avoiding the "F" word. Arguably, the more progressive readings of these programs might also be lost—they would now be, simply, programs for yuppie women. For example, during the 1992 rebroadcast of *thirtysomething,* a promo ran repeatedly that made an incredible, tongue-in-cheek, point-by-point comparison between *China Beach* and *L.A. Law* "back to back on Lifetime." The promo stated that both shows deal with "life's little problems." The fact that *China Beach* was a "woman's show" that dealt with blood, war, and death in an often grimly serious manner was lost on Lifetime, whose promo also implied that *L.A. Law* was a sex comedy only one step up from *Three's Company* (or rather, they knew the difference but chose to cover it over with pomo irony).

When *L.A. Law* started on Lifetime, it was marketed as a woman's program full of beefy men. In its own publicity, Lifetime claims to "deliver the most consistent, most desirable women demographics, and compensate[s] for broadcasting under-delivery." Lifetime also syndicated two of the handful of yuppie shows to make the list of top-rated programs for the Reagan era: *Moonlighting* and *L.A. Law*. Clearly their appeal to a larger audience as well as to upscale women makes them unique.[4] Eventually, all of the feminist "quality" shows of the 1980s reemerged on Lifetime: *Molly Dodd, Cagney and Lacey, Kay O'Brien, Heartbeat,* and *China Beach*.

In 1992 Lifetime ran promos for *L.A. Law* and *China Beach* within an episode of *thirtysomething* in which Dana Delaney (pre-*China Beach* but now post-*China Beach*) plays a woman with whom Gary has fallen in love. As if in vengeance, the husband of a casual lover has trashed Gary's apartment and written death threats on the walls. As he and the woman played by *China Beach*'s Dana Delaney look on in horror, Lifetime cuts to a promo for *L.A. Law*. The next commercial break links a scene in which Gary fantasizes the Dana Delaney character has stabbed him in the back with a scissors after a discussion of trust and fidelity (qualities notably lacking in Gary) to a promo for *China Beach* on Lifetime in which McMurphy (Dana Delaney) discusses men with the prostitute and the USO entertainer under the promo's male voice announcing "the women of China Beach." Actually, the conversation is created by Lifetime's editing of the promo, as K. C. appears to be excerpted from a different episode than the other two. In an uncanny example of female bonding across space, time, and texts, the next segment of *thirtysomething* features a "hen fest" between the Dana Delaney character, Hope, and Nancy in which a discussion of the male of the species—"It's either Nietschze or Pee Wee Herman—there's no middle ground"—uncannily parallels the promo for *China Beach* (the three women talking) that we just viewed: "Only Lifetime gives you the women of China Beach—on men:" a series of clips—McMurphy: "Men are whatever we make them." K. C.: "I know what they want and I give it to them." USO entertainer: "If he doesn't belch in public, you're sure it's love."

Lifetime gives these three yuppie shows—*thirtysomething, L.A. Law,* and *China Beach*—the opportunity to appear as a unified textual field with interpenetrating boundaries not possible in their original network broadcasts. Lifetime, in the nineties, has recreated yuppie TV of the eighties in a kind of yuppie nostalgia channel, the eighties equivalent of Nick at Nite for baby boomers. Nick re-creates our childhood,

Lifetime our young adulthood. Lifetime also rewrites all of these programs as women's texts.

It also claims to "deliver" the "highest concentration of working women among the basic cable networks in key dayparts." The "Lifetime Viewer Product Usage Profile" tells advertisers that Lifetime women score high in the following categories: rented a car, own credit cards, purchased aerobic fitness shoes, traveled by plane, purchased tailored suits, own money market fund and purchased luxury car, as well as more mundane consumer achievements (*Advertising Age* 1989). This profile places the audience, at least in part, solidly within the yuppie mainstream.

The Yuppie Spectator

The percentage of unsuccessful yuppie shows indicates that, even during the 1980s, the mass audience still held sway for network TV. As we have seen, estimates of the number of yuppies in the population range from 1.5 million to 20 million depending on whom you include. The truly elite group at the lower end of this range was too small to constitute an audience for 1980s network TV. Even the least successful yuppie programs, *Jack and Mike* and *Hometown* (which averaged about a 7.5 rating on the Nielsen scale, with a 12 share each), drew about 6 million households; assuming a yuppie household to consist of two unmarried adults (dinks), this would mean 12 million yuppies would be needed to constitute a totally yup audience pool for these programs.

For purposes of comparison, on a good week (7 March 1989), the moderately successful *thirtysomething* drew about 14 million households, compared to the hit series *The Wonder Years* at about 21 million and *Roseanne* at 26 million households (*Variety* 1989, p. 41).[5]

Advertisers were wary both of yuppie marketing and of trying to reach yuppies through TV. Since yuppies are small in number and fickle in taste, major corporations found them too risky a target. Moreover, yuppies were too busy to watch much TV. Therefore American Express found magazines and newspapers more effective than television for reaching the yuppie vanguard (*Newsweek* 1984b, p. 29). Even though *Hill Street Blues* (1981–1987) was the first TV program to be sponsored by Mercedes-Benz, more than two-thirds of the advertising on that show in the early 1980s consisted of traditional ads for traditional products advertised on TV (toothpaste, hair products, food products). Only a small number of the ads featured representations of yuppie culture. For example, looking at an arc of four shows from spring 1982 (the

"Captain Freedom" episodes), it is striking just how many mass audience products are advertised: Johnson's baby powder, the Dodge 400 and Aries K automobiles, Black Flag roach killer, Dentyne gum, vitamins, Bell phones, Cling-Free, Wendy's, McDonald's, Pizza Hut, JC Penney, Dixie Cups, Honda bikes, Bud Light, Woolite, a hemorrhoid product, Clairol Nice n' Easy, hair conditioners and home perms, toothpaste, mouthwash, Skin Bracer, bubble bath, and potato chips. The ads for yuppie products or those addressing a yuppie spectator are rarer: two for Kronenberg beer ("Europe's number one beer"), Bank of America Travelers Cheques, and the Prudential are upscale in appeal and presentation. Two brands of foreign car are advertised—Toyota and the Volkswagen Quantum—but the appeals are not markedly different from other car ads. A few other ads try for yuppie images, although the products themselves are ones no yuppie would touch: Gallo wines, Martini and Rossi Asti Spumante, and Foster Grant sunglasses. Later in the decade, however, a program such as *Moonlighting*—a mass audience hit, not just a demographic one—is littered with calls to a yuppie spectator if not to the yuppie audience alone. For example, the *Moonlighting* and *thirtysomething* season premieres in December 1988 (the latter analyzed in Chapter 4) were strewn with images of baby boomers in their commercials (*PC Week* 1988).

Even though ad after ad during the *Moonlighting* opener featured healthy, affluent baby boomers, only one commercial truly embodied the yuppie stereotype I have been describing. "Nissan wants you to succeed in business," a powerful male voice tells us, as a group of yuppie corporate types (one female) dressed in black and dark gray power suits exits a Wall Street building and fits easily into the sleek black car. The commercial develops an elaborate analogy between certain business terminology and the art of driving, all the while following the black Maxima from Wall Street to the Ferry as it enacts "the conference room," "executive decision making," "client entertainment," "risk management," and a "hostile takeover" of another sleek sedan. As they unload at the Ferry, the announcer intones, "This real world business course was brought to you by Maxima—the four-door sports car." The logo appears: "Nissan: Built for the Human Race." The obvious pun on "race" points to the emphasis placed on competition and individualism in the yuppie image. But this was only one commercial out of twenty-five that were broadcast during *Moonlighting*. Two of the commercials went for an even more upscale—ruling class but definitely not yuppie—appeal: a Cadillac spot that featured a lawn party right out of

Brideshead Revisited and a steeplechase, and the well-known spot for Forever Krystle (described in Chapter 6).

The *thirtysomething* premiere had images of old-money wealth (Cadillac again), a yuppie stockbroker taking Actifed, funky characters à la Melissa taking spontaneous photos with a Kodak Impulse camera; parents giving McDonald's gift certificates for Christmas, thin yuppies with babies eating pure, natural dairy butter (only 36 calories), and so on. Once again, the true yuppie images were in the minority. As late as 1988, the Television Bureau of Advertising was still trying to convince the industry to use more television to reach baby boomers (Smythe 1988, p. 23).

Compare the above ads to a string of ads just after the credits during a "*thirtysomething* episode on Lifetime": a suited woman is told by her father to go right to the top for answers (Valu-Rite Pharmacy); "Life is short; play hard": a Reebok "I believe" ad;[6] an ad for packaged pasta that comes with a pasta and wine guide that turns your home into a yuppie restaurant; Yoplait yogurt—"low fat, calcium rich, with active yogurt cultures . . . it's something forty-year-old Vicky Gentry does every day . . . creamy, rich, do it for you" (images of woman athlete); a promo by Corbin Bernsen for *L.A. Law*—"the law, it's here on Lifetime television." This cuts directly to an image of a bride in a wedding veil that Melissa is photographing with Shakespeare's Sonnet 29 read over it from Gary's lecture. Lifetime rewrites the beginning of the episode to flow into the stream of ads. The flow links statements about the richness of yogurt, pasta, wine and self-actualization through exercise to what might have been a very different sort of commentary on the relationship of art to life. Not only does the Lifetime broadcast of *thirtysomething* create nostalgia for the sixties; it creates nostalgia for the eighties as well by re-creating the decade's images in its commercials. Specifically, it creates nostalgia in upscale female baby boomers for that affluent time before parenthood and the recession. In a way, it is always 1984 on Lifetime. It's just that, demographically speaking, 1984 didn't reach television until 1992.

Thus during the Reagan years the major networks were not so much interested in "pure" yuppie demographics as they were in constructing yuppie *spectators* for advertising (i. e. getting baby boomers and others to agree to be positioned/interpellated as yuppies). Fredric Jameson, *Newsweek,* and demographers agree that the influence of yuppies exceeded their numbers. According to *Newsweek*: "What enhances the importance of being Yuppie is that they sit on top of the largest, richest, best-educated generation ever born. . . . Even those who don't meet all the statistical criteria may find their lives and spending habits to a large degree falling into patterns set by the Yuppies" (1984b, p. 28).

Notes

1 According to Marissa Piesman, coauthor with Marilee Hartley of *The Yuppie Handbook* (1984), the term can be traced back to Chicago, but she places its origins much earlier, sometime in the late 1970s (Piesman 1993).

2 A significant finding in the demographic literature is that the baby boom overall experienced a significant loss of economic power in the 1980s. See Michael X. Delli Carpini 1986, p. 266. This finding is corroborated by Paul C. Light, who writes: "Even adding the baby boomers who try to look and buy like yuppies — the 'would be's' as advertisers call them — roughly 60 million baby boomers do not fit this picture. Thus, there are four baby boomers at or below the poverty line for every yuppie far above it. . . . In 1985, four out of ten baby boomers made less than $10,000 a year, making them roughly eight times as numerous as the yuppies (1988, p.21). Light also tells us, "In 1984, 34 percent of the baby boomers borrowed money to supplement their incomes, 30 percent put off medical care because of the economy and almost half looked for a new job or part-time work to make ends meet" (p. 198).

3 *Return of the Secaucus 7* (1980) was an earlier prototype, yet it was the phrase "Big Chill generation" from the more mainstream film that stuck.

4 According to Brooks and Marsh *Moonlighting* ranged from number 9 to number 24 in 1985 – 1987. *L. A. Law* tied *Moonlighting* for number 12 in 1987 – 1988. The only other top-rated yuppie shows during the Reagan years were *Hill Street Blues* (number 21 in 1982 – 1983), *Miami Vice* (number 9 in 1985 – 1986), and *The Wonder Years* (number 10 for 1987 – 1988) (1988, p. 975).

5 Based on approximately ninety million TV households in 1989 (Nielsen data provided to author). Actual ratings and shares given in *Variety* are *thirtysomething* (16.1/28); *The Wonder Years* (22.4/33), and *Roseanne* (27.7/40).

6 The full text of the commercial goes: "You are what you believe [over images of exercising women]. I believe babe is a four-letter word. I believe that the person who said winning isn't everything never won anything. I believe sweat is sexy. I don't believe in liposuction. I don't believe blondes have more fun. I believe in mass transit. I believe you should go big or stay home. I believe there's an athlete in all of us." Title: "Life is short; play hard."

3

Yuppie Envy and Yuppie Guilt:

L.A. Law and *thirtysomething*

Yuppies could not during the Reagan years be successfully *directly* represented on network TV. Since the true yuppie image is a comic parody and especially considering no one will admit to being one, it is doubtful that a serious portrait of yuppie characters, cast in the sober image of *The Yuppie Handbook* and the *Newsweek* cover story, or, like Jackie and Mike, suffering no guilt over their gentrified condos and gleaming kitchens (echoing the unreconstructed yuppie in the *Newsweek* story who owned $1,200 worth of pots and pans but ate every meal in restaurants), would have been successful even in a narrowcasting format.

In the summer of 1991, the popular press saw *Regarding Henry* and *The Doctor* as yuppie guilt trips in which formerly driven and materialistic professional men rediscover spiritual values. In these post-yuppie male melodramas of redemption through suffering, an attorney and a surgeon, respectively, reshape their identities as a consequence of devastating illnesses that serve as metaphors for compromised idealism. The term "yuppie" is never mentioned but functions as a subtext for everything that was wrong with the lives of these successful men. Two crimes emerge, one public and one private. Each man has put the demands of professionalism ahead of the needs of those he serves. And each man has neglected wife and family in an obsessive devotion to career (a hallmark of the 1980s yuppie image). These films of the early 1990s were seen as marking a shift away from the glorification of yuppie values in the film and television of the Reagan years; indeed they were viewed as pop cultural markers of the beginning of a new age. Such a view assumes that yuppie guilt is a post-Reagan phenomenon.

Yet I would argue that the thematics of yuppie guilt started much earlier, as early as, say, *The Big Chill* (1983). Furthermore, yuppie guilt is not an aftermath of yuppie values but a constitutive part of them. If yuppie envy permeated the advertising on *L.A. Law* and *thirtysome-*

thing, it was yuppie guilt that permeated the narratives. What are yuppies guilty about? According to *The Big Chill*, it is their material and financial success, their compromised ideals, and, for the women, their lost opportunities for love and children. Thus we find a group of baby boomers (already thirtysomething in 1983) lamenting the death by suicide of their sixties comrade, the only one to retain hippie values into the eighties. The others represent various baby boomer subject positions—indeed the characters are little more than ideological stick figures. There's the childless female corporate attorney, the running shoe manufacturer, the TV cop show actor, the writer for *People* magazine. As low as the others have sunk, nothing could be lower than starring in a weekly TV series. As the former campus radical turned TV detective confides to the *People* writer in a heart-to-heart vignette directly following the dance in the kitchen, "I think I've just been too slow to realize that people our own age, histories just like ours, having gone through all the same stuff, could be dishonest, unprincipled, backstabbing sleaze balls." When his cynical comrade responds, "I could've told you that a long time ago," the TV heartthrob continues, "Yeah, well, I was prejudiced in their favor. I thought because they looked like us and talked like us, they were gonna think like us." The evocation of yuppie guilt is exacerbated by the sixties tunes blaring on the soundtrack—even the music was better then. But, of course, it's nostalgia laced with guilt, and no one's about to give up materialism in 1983. In this way, *The Big Chill* set the pattern for all the yuppie shows to follow: create envy for the lifestyles of the characters while at the same time creating guilt over their compromised values. This pattern permeates yuppie shows all the way up to the Steadmans' ever unfinished but well-appointed kitchen, where the clan gathers on *thirtysomething*.

Yuppie guilt permeates the first successful TV programs actually labeled "yuppie" by the popular upscale media: *L.A. Law* (1986–1994) and *thirtysomething* (1987–1991). Whereas *American Film* comes right out and says *thirtysomething* is "a show written by yuppies, about yuppies, for yuppies" (Lantos 1987, p. 50), *New York* magazine, practically a house organ for Manhattan yuppie culture, codes the same thought by saying, "It's by baby-boomers, about baby-boomers, and for baby-boomers" (Hoban 1988, p. 48). In a fashion typical of the self-denial that defines yuppiedom, the same article only uses the yup word when citing those who disapprove of the show's whining: Elvis Mitchell, a TV and film critic for National Public Radio, calls the show "a bunch of white people sitting around whining." He continues, "I've never seen such a blatant pitch to demographics outside Saturday morning TV."

"Simply put, it's yuppie television," says one Y-person. "It represents everything regrettable about the life we live" (Hoban 1988, p. 50).

Indeed, as with yuppie self-parody, it would seem as if the nonguilty yuppies were always them not us. Guilt and self-loathing, I argue, are symptoms of TV yuppiedom rather than representing its aftermath. But yuppie representations on TV were designed to evoke a more complex response in the spectator they constructed. The spectator was supposed to experience both envy and guilt at the same time. Since envy is more easily evoked by visual images and guilt conveyed by narrative, it was easy to split the hoped-for responses between the two channels of meaning: visuals and story. Unsuccessfully in *Jack and Mike* and *Heartbeat*, successfully in *L.A. Law*, the look of the show is played against its story lines. To put it more academically, the visual codes—the mise-en-scène—are juxtaposed with the narrational codes. This links the yuppie shows to postmodern shows like *Miami Vice*, whose heavy-handed, disjunctive, moralistic plots were overlaid with the pink and lime hues of tropical deco. When critics—and possibly some audience members—read *L.A. Law* as a yuppie show, they were responding to the look of the show (and of its yuppie commercials) with envy. This reading appears to have overpowered other possible readings based on the narrative undercutting of the yuppie visuals. *L.A. Law* as TV commercial for lala land wins out over the socially conscious "quality" show in this reading.

The more successful programs that have been labeled "yuppie shows" do not really represent yuppie culture directly; nor do they aim necessarily to flatter a yuppie audience. Programs such as *Hill Street Blues* and *St. Elsewhere* in the early to mid-1980s and *L.A. Law* and *thirtysomething* in the latter part of the decade understood that audience hostility to yuppie culture needed to be defused. Although direct representations of yuppie culture might have worked well in TV advertising, the television program had to maintain at least an illusion that it was more than merely a sales pitch.

Along these lines, it is interesting that the yuppie shows, the "quality TV" of the early 1980s, eschewed yuppie representations almost entirely except for in the commercials. *Hill Street Blues* and *St. Elsewhere* went after baby boomer demographics with the iconography of inner-city poverty, not urban affluence. Yuppie spectator positions were created indirectly, through a certain kind of narrative and through the commercials. These landmark quality shows addressed a yuppie spectator through a modernist art discourse (see Chapter 4) and through a displaced appeal to baby boomer ideals of the 1960s. Specifically, they addressed the failure of liberal institutions from a baby boomer rather than a Right populist perspective as had the made-for-TV movies, for surveys showed that the majority of baby boomers remained liberal on social issues: "Even after giving Reagan huge majorities in 1980 and 1984, they were still unwilling to abandon their social concerns. However, they were not overwhelmed with confidence about government's effectiveness in addressing poverty either" (Light 1988, p. 233). It was those institutions designed to serve the underclass that are seen to have failed, even though the large ensemble casts are shown struggling against the tide. In each program, a patriarchal figure (Furillo in *Hill Street Blues*, Westphall in *St. Elsewhere*) upholds the ideals of the past against a configuration of forces representative of what Todd Gitlin calls the "post-liberal shading to neo-conservative" ethos of the ensemble cast. For instance, a crisis of faith comes for public defender Joyce Davenport when a black female colleague is killed in the line of duty.

Similarly, in the pilot episode of *Northern Exposure*, the yuppie greed of Dr. Fleischman is tempered by the frontier values of Cicely, Alaska, in the first post-Reagan quality show hit. Significantly, both *Northern Exposure* (first telecast 12 July 1990) and the cult show *Twin Peaks* (8 April 1990 – 10 June 1991) remove themselves from television's urban and Sunbelt settings of the eighties to northwestern frontier towns. The antimaterialist iconography of the western returns as an antidote to the eighties. Sandwiched between these programming strategies of appealing to the quality audience without using yuppie representations, we find the "decade" of the yuppie, spanning the Reagan years of 1983 to about 1988. Only then was it okay to visualize yuppie culture on TV. Even so, the images had to be tempered by narratives of guilt.

L.A. Law

The *L.A. Law* pilot opens on Arnold Becker driving to work on the freeway in his fancy sports car.[1] But the real commercial for the yuppie lifestyle occurs during the second season, in the winter of 1988, and again features Arnie as icon. This precredits segment is typical in that it focuses on a vignette from the life of one character somewhat detached from the rest of the show. This segment is followed by the ritual of the credits and the weekly meeting of the firm that corresponds to roll call on *Hill Street Blues*. Yet the segment is unusual in its visual style — cut to a driving beat exactly like a yuppie lifestyle ad, quite like the car ad Todd Gitlin describes as typical of the mid-eighties:

The advertising agencies began to conceive of a new generation of ads designed to—in their language "respond to the new Japanese challenge." They spoke of "lifestyle," "image," cars that "forge an identity" and "make a statement." They decided, in other words, to repel the Japanese invaders in a particular way, consonant with a larger ideological mood: thus, the pure thrust of the new ad, offering aggression, liberation, streamlining, and a portentous pseudospirituality all at once. It says, "We're ready for you if you're man enough for us." It is lean and clean; it carries no extra inches of fat; it works out; it sings; once again, a song of the open road.

Most of all, the new-style car commercial reveals something about the new-style man who has been pronounced fit to drive into the future. . . . He is man on the move, man ready to go anywhere. . . . The ideal man of the commercials embodies, in short, the master fantasy of the Reagan era: the fantasy of thrusting, self-sufficient man, cutting loose, free of gravity, free of attachments. (1987, p. 143)

In short, the new man of the car commercials is Arnold Becker. In an episodic sequence, we see Arnie getting ready for work on a beautiful Los Angeles morning, a typical structure for a 1980s commercial (influenced by the rhythmic cutting to the music and narrative discontinuity feeding back and forth from ads to music videos). We see him on his rowing machine and then his exercycle against the perfectly framed ocean backdrop. The reverse angle finds Arnie diving into his pool as the camera moves laterally with him, displaying a perfect view of his Richard Meier–like all-white high modernist house. As he emerges from the water gasping with pleasure, a direct cut takes us to a close-up of his juicer in the white tile kitchen. As Arnie squeezes fresh oranges while grooving to the beat of the nondiegetic music on the soundtrack, a wider view reveals a kitchen island with portable TV; we cut to a close-up of the TV screen showing a man shoveling snow somewhere (not L.A.). Arnie drinks the juice with gusto, once again as in a commercial for yuppie-lifestyle products, showing the yuppie actually using the products. A jump cut takes him into the bedroom, where he removes every last bit of lint from his Hugo Boss suit. We view the tiled jacuzzi bath framed with vertical blinds by the ocean-view window; to complete the picture, the camera picks up a reflection of the shower in the dressing room mirror; a sexy female voice calls out, "Don't ding my Jag getting into your car." Next we see Arnie getting into his white Porsche parked next to the red Jaguar. He inserts the key into the igni-

tion in a phallic penetrating gesture shot in close-up. The music drives on as he pulls out and down the canyon road.

The music ends here in a series of drumrolls, but the vignette isn't over. In a tableau of a very different sort, Arnie arrives at the office and extols the virtues of California life to his secretary, Roxanne. She in turn responds: "I was woken up by a dumpster. The only thing to nestle up to me in the last eight months is currently in the slammer for stock fraud. My bagel was so stale I practically chipped a tooth. I'm retaining water and I'm all out of Midol. Is life figured out here, you ask?" And she gives him the raspberry. Fade to black, the *L.A. Law* theme blares up and the trunk comes down on yet another episode.

Here we find juxtaposed a commercial for the California version of the yuppie lifestyle and a reminder that class and gender conflict were exacerbated in the eighties. In fact the tone of the ad is somewhat satirical with Arnie at his shallow, materialistic, peacocky worst. We wonder if the entire "music video" sequence isn't some kind of parody, and the scene with Roxanne convinces us it must have been. In this type of narrative, each position taken is qualified by another. Roxanne voices the response of the mass audience when she reminds Arnie that his upward mobility is at the expense of her downward mobility. At the same time, we get to experience the visual pleasure of Arnie's perfect lifestyle without having to feel that we are entering into yuppie greed, for it is Roxanne as everywoman who gets the last gesture.

L.A. Law at first glance seems to be the best example on TV of a successful representation of yuppie culture—the corporate wardrobes, the plush offices, the fancy cars, the stylish restaurants—all of which even figure in the narrative: Arnie worries when a prospective client disparages his clothes; Arnie takes Bennie shopping for clothes right out of the Tweeds catalogue rather than the Goodwill racks; Victor's fancy car is repeatedly vandalized; and Stuart, Anne, and Arnie fight like children for possession of the late Chaney's large office. But the culture portrayed is also just L.A. the land of heedless wealth familiar to film and TV viewers for generations. It does not precisely fit the "urban," Wall Street part of the yuppie construct portrayed in *Newsweek* and *The Yuppie Handbook*. Even if the "look" of the show is readable as yuppie, the narrative strategy sets out a careful balancing act in which yuppie values are played out against traditional or even 1960s values and found to be wanting. As Judith Mayne has written in regard to the show's feminism, "The door swings both ways" (1988, p. 33).

Haynes Johnson, in his generally negative review of the Reagan years, finds reason for hope in that the "yuppies" represent "a generation imbued both with fiscal conservatism and practicality and with social liberalism and individual tolerance" (1991, p. 473). It is to the latter two values that the narratives of *L.A. Law* appeal, rather than to the self-serving greed of the publicly constructed yuppie image. Frequently characters have to defend the system of corporate greed, but they feel guilty for doing so and often cross over in some way by their actions. At least through 1987, the cases portrayed tended to take a high moral ground; even when representing corporate clients, an attorney like Anne Kelsey is able to take a righteous stand against the firm's clients, as in the story arc involving toxic waste by her own client, a water company. When Kelsey goes up against an insurance company in a *pro bono* case, she feels guilty that she cared more about winning than about her client. Even the handsome top-billed couple at the center of the legal narratives—Michael Kuzak and Grace van Owen—describe themselves in a telling moment as "grim and humorless." Kuzak even identifies with witnesses whose interests he must work against, as in the ninety-minute pilot episode, where his client is the arrogant rich teenager who raped a dying black woman. In the "Sid Hirschberg" story arc, Kuzak identifies with his friend and fellow attorney even when Sid's inability to cope with the legal system results in a dramatic slow-motion suicide. Although the yuppie image stresses success, early episodes of *L.A. Law* were as much about the dignity of failure. Many of the show's most appealing supporting characters began as losers: Bennie, Sid Hirschberg, Dave Myer, Roxanne, the Salamander, law associates Abigail Perkins and Tony Giannelli (who is unable to pass the bar exam and has to rejoin his family's circus act and be shot out of a cannon). Even partners Douglas Brackman and Arnold Becker are frequently portrayed as buffoons. Douglas, in his mid-forties is a pre-yuppie corporate type, a failed son and husband. Yet his most significant story line in terms of yuppie values is his trial for being a slumlord and consequent guilt feelings—for Douglas, it was an investment—he had no idea conditions were so bad. But it is fascinating that the most yuppie of the characters, Arnie Becker, should continually be portrayed as something of a fool.

When age is mentioned on the show, it places the main characters on the Big Chill side of the baby boom—both Anne Kelsey and Arnie Becker are said to be thirty-six years old during the 1986–1987 first season, and Douglas Brackman is forty-four. In a similar vein, *thirtysomething* stresses the participation of its characters in 1960s politics, when it is obvious the actors are too young to have participated. The show even flashes back to the characters in their hippie incarnations. The characters of Gary and later Susannah stand as place markers for the social-activist, hippie lifestyle, identifications that are available to the spectator even if, as some believe, the text condemns them. Although the second half of the baby boom never had this history, it is invoked by these programs in order to harness liberal social sentiments for purposes of identification against yuppie greed. Barbara Ehrenreich (1989, p. 198) points out that yuppies are sometimes portrayed as children of the sixties and sometimes as the children of the sixties' children (e.g., Alex Keaton of *Family Ties*). This would seem to be contradictory, but only if you view TV images of yuppies as historically accurate and unselfconscious rather than as symbolic ideological constructs. The sleight of hand regarding age has the effect of collapsing the baby boom time span into a single multifaceted image. The yuppie construct needs both sides, both generations—the one in order to produce the advertising stereotype, the other in order to produce the guilt.

Thus I would argue that *L.A. Law*, at least in its early seasons, which took place during the Reagan era, has much more in common with the earlier 1980s quality dramas *Hill Street Blues* and *St. Elsewhere* than it does with the "failed" yuppie shows like *Jack and Mike. L.A. Law* began in continuity with the heroic tradition of these shows about baby boomers struggling, often nobly, against dying institutions such as urban police stations and public hospitals. Yet *L.A. Law* plays out to its dénouement the MTM family of coworkers concept that infused the Bochco shows and their spinoffs during the decade. The quality TV tradition of the family of coworkers transformed easily into the work-obsessed yuppie value system of the eighties. Leland McKenzie is the last of the MTM-style patriarchs that began with Lou Grant in 1970 but really blossomed a bit later in the ensemble dramas *Lou Grant, Hill Street Blues,* and *St. Elsewhere.* The events at the end of the 1991 season (the near breakup of the firm) seemed more out of *Dynasty* than the warmer families of quality TV, yet we seemed to be able to take this kind of venom on *L.A. Law* just after its charms had seemingly expired on the campier prime time soaps. Just as *Dallas* was reliving its past in the final episode, *L.A. Law* and *thirtysomething* were taking over its familial material.

thirtysomething

If *L.A. Law* operates by splitting the channels into different codes so that yuppie envy and yuppie guilt operate simultaneously in the consciousness of the target audience, *thirtysomething* pursues a slightly different strategy, accounting for its very different look, tone, and atmosphere.[2] *thirtysomething,* that is, creates an aesthetic out of yuppie guilt. Envy recedes into the background and reemerges in the form of the show's own commercials and product merchandising. Within the narrative, during its brief Reagan-era run (fall 1987 to spring 1988 with a couple of episodes in December 1988), envy was reserved for the yuppie nuclear family of Michael, Hope, and Janie. All of the other characters envied them. But starting in January 1989, fortunes started to reverse, and by the time the show was canceled in May 1991, Hope and Michael were no longer enviable. For the audience, it is doubtful that envy was ever the kind of visual stimulant evoked by *Dynasty, L.A. Law,* and *Miami Vice.* Instead *thirtysomething* expresses self-loathing both at the narrative and audience response levels. *thirtysomething* appears to have focused the scorn all baby boomers held for the yuppie stereotype, often being referred to in the press as "the show you love to hate" and being chided for the "whining" of its characters. The morning after ABC canceled *thirtysomething* (29 May 1991), *Good Morning, America* ran a

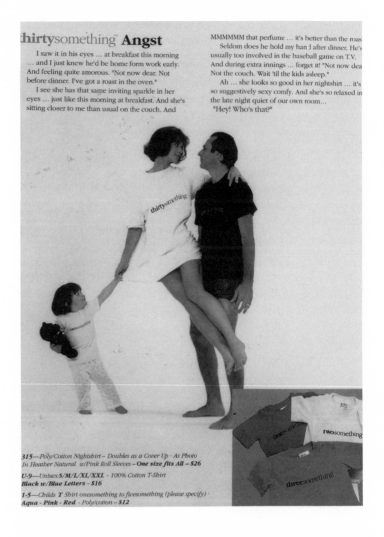

hirtysomething **Angst**

I saw it in his eyes … at breakfast this morning … and I just knew he'd be home form work early. And feeling quite amorous. "Not now dear. Not before dinner. I've got a roast in the oven."

I see she has that same inviting sparkle in her eyes … just like this morning at breakfast. And she's sitting closer to me than usual on the couch. And

MMMMMM that perfume … it's better than the roast Seldom does he hold my hand after dinner. He's usually too involved in the baseball game on T.V. And during extra innings … forget it! "Not now dear Not the couch. Wait 'til the kids asleep."

Ah … she looks so good in her nightshirt … it's so suggestively sexy comfy. And she's so relaxed in the late night quiet of our own room…

"Hey! Who's that?"

*315—Poly/Cotton Nightshirt – Doubles as a Cover Up · As Photo In Heather Natural w/Pink Roll Sleeves – **One size fits All – $26***

*U-9—Unisex **S/M/L/XL/XXL** - 100% Cotton T-Shirt **Black w/Blue Letters - $16***

*1-5—Childs **T** Shirt onesomething to fivesomething (please specify) · **Aqua - Pink - Red** - Poly/cotton – $12*

eulogy that captured the spectrum of audience opinion on the show. In a series of on-the-street interviews with New York viewers, it becomes clear that the selection of fans interviewed is far from arbitrary—many of them appear to be dead ringers for the character types on the show itself. To the question "How do you feel about the cancellation of *thirtysomething*?" the following replies are given:

> Oh well, so much for whining yuppies. (woman yuppie)

> I found it a very depressing show. Every episode seemed to have some kind of gloom in it and Hope always seemed so depressed all the time. (Hope-alike woman with infant)

I have no problem with the cancellation of *thirtysomething*. Girl-friend makes me watch it. Kill it. (twentysomething man)

Unfortunately there's not too much serious watching on TV. They take this away and there's going to be even less. (a thirtysomething man in a suit)

I liked the show. I thought it was real life. (young woman yuppie)

I'm depressed about the cancellation. I enjoyed watching it and I'm saddened. (Melissa-alike)

Maybe it'll come back. (man in baseball cap)

As in articles about the show, those who considered it "real life" and those who considered it "yuppievision" never used the other's language in speaking of the program. *thirtysomething* creators Edward Zwick and Marshall Herskovitz always denied that their characters were yuppies: " 'Yes, Hope and Michael have a nice, big old house,' says Zwick of his centerpiece couple on *thirtysomething*. 'But it's in terrible disrepair and they can't afford to fix it up' " (Minsky 1987, pp. 41–42). Since early episodes of the series contradict this view (they attempt to fix it up, but they feel guilty about being able to afford things), the creators' quote reflects not an "accurate" evaluation of the Steadmans' image, but rather, the producers' clever understanding of the negative connotations of the term "yuppie." Just as yuppie *New York* magazine knew to use the term "baby boomer" in lieu of "yuppie," early episodes of *thirtysomething* knew how to play on the audience's yuppie guilt by ascribing it to the characters and thematizing it in the scripts. Indeed the series began as a kind of meditation on yuppie guilt in which the yup word itself is invoked and denied. "The show you love to hate" strategy succeeds because yuppies are the baby boomers you love to hate—but never, never oneself—not for Michael Steadman and not for the target demographic audience either. In fact, *thirtysomething* started out as a Bergmanesque *Big Chill*. The first three episodes had extended references to the Steadmans' yuppie status, with the third episode actually using the yup word in a horror/fantasy sequence from Michael Steadman's point of view. The pilot obfuscates the exact ages of the thirtysomethings. In fact, they seem younger than some of the references imply. Melissa is thirty-one in 1987, meaning she was born in 1956. We later learn that Michael is two years older than Melissa, with Hope and Ellen a year younger than Michael (meaning he would have been born in 1954 and Hope and Ellen in 1955). This makes them rather young for the references to Woodstock and tear gas in parks, and decisions their parents made in 1946. The idea is for *thirtysomething* to encompass both early and later baby boomers: the first wave with its radical politics and countercultural lifestyles, the second wave with values more easily assimilated back into the mainstream.

The entire first episode plays with oblique references to yuppie culture while ostensibly thematizing the Steadmans' guilt and fear of adulthood. In a flashback, we view Hope and Ellen as yuppie career women discussing Michael at a fern bar lunch. Michael is appalled by the cost of a yuppie-brand baby carriage. The Steadmans' kitchen is decidedly not out of *Jack and Mike:* there is stuff pasted all over the refrigerator, the wallpaper is peeling, the breakfast nook is unfinished and remains so for at least two seasons. The Michael and Elliot Company office with its glass block pomo open design is much more amenable to the *Met Home* aesthetic, but within it Michael fights with a client over issues of integrity while Elliot makes jokes about needing to earn a living. When Hope has to bring the baby to a restaurant lunch with Ellen, the event inaugurates the second wave of yuppiedom: parenthood. This is what *thirtysomething* will commemorate: the messy, "sticky" house, the angst over the need to be a breadwinner, the sacrificing of career for motherhood. "I crawled back to Teller today. I sold out," Michael tells Hope while the more realistic Elliot refers to the "two wives three kids four cars two mortgages." "I hate people who talk like this. I know we're lucky," Michael finally confesses. But he will continue to "talk like this" for quite a while.

The early scenes of the second episode (6 October 1987) find the Steadmans' house in total disarray. Gary has to fix the torn-up bathroom in time for the visit of Hope's parents—the first in a long chain of coming-to-terms-with-our-parents, coming-of-age narratives for the thirtysomethings. Despite the producers' protests, isn't a house in the process of renovation the ultimate yuppie dream à la *Met Home?* The episode contrasts the Steadmans' values with the more traditional good housekeeping of the parental generation. But is this a moral or a marketing crisis? Meanwhile, the episode shows Gary in his faculty office, a representative of values seen as opposed to consumerism.

To this point the ostensible theme of the program has been the crisis of parenthood and the inevitable adult responsibilities it brings to a heedless generation. The third episode (13 October 1987) will situate this discourse specifically within the realm of yuppiedom. For this reason, I will be giving it the most attention. Episode 3 begins with the archetypal yuppie narrative of rehabbing one's house; it ends with a celebration of a new kind of family. In between, we finally encounter the yup word.

In a typical narrative strategy, the episode parallels a domestic with a professional situation that can be unified thematically. In this case, the domestic situation is the rehabbing of the breakfast room in time for a housewarming celebration coupled with the need for Michael Steadman to fire his incompetent secretary in time to rent a soundstage on which to shoot a commercial for the ethically shady account they've agreed to take on. No wonder this episode focuses on Michael Steadman's personal crisis of faith—not over his failures but rather over his success in two areas crucial to defining the yuppie lifestyle: urban gentrification and self-fulfilling careerism. Of course it's the latter that makes the former possible—hence Michael's guilt. These twin spheres of yuppiedom become fixed by two visual images: the perennially unfinished Steadman kitchen and the chic postmodern open space of the Michael and Elliot Company. These will be the sets where most of the interactions take place during the first season of the show; in the winter of 1989, near the beginning of the second season, the office space is replaced by the more corporate but still playful and postmodern offices of Miles Drentell's D.A.A., a cubicled Peewee's Playhouse for adults.

The narrative commences—typically—with the kitchen set, as Hope and Michael are sorting out the boxes of their youth, filled with Hendrix and Jefferson Airplane albums. "We moved into this house in November and we're still in boxes." Michael takes up the task of finishing the breakfast room, for him a symbol of nuclear family happiness. A young, hunky independent contractor comes to give estimates on built-ins; the entire atmosphere is reminiscent of the many contemporaneous chronicles of rehabbing featured in the annals of *Metropolitan Home*, up to and including an article on how remodeling your kitchen can place a strain on your marriage. As in *Met Home*, remodeling is an existential activity. As Michael puts it, "I'm depressed about the impossibility of ever having anything in your life exactly the way it's supposed to be." What Michael wants to do—but confesses to Melissa he feels guilty about—is to throw a huge networking/housewarming party about which he's eager but cynical. As I've argued, this cynicism toward their values is part of the yuppie sensibility as it is anchored in the narratives of *thirtysomething* for the late 1980s; the Steadmans are not the unselfconscious yups of the 1984 *Newsweek* cover story. The *Newsweek* article permits *Met Home* subscribers to define themselves as too cynical and too politically correct to be yuppie. Yet *Met Home* and *thirtysomething* with their combination of political correctness and materialism are the true yuppie culture. In this way, *thirtysomething* both reflects and recreates the image of the yuppie at the end of the Reagan era, after the 1987 stock market crash, which soon will affect Michael and Elliot as well.

For Michael and Elliot earn their daily bread by that ultimate selling out of hippie values: making TV commercials. No wonder Michael's nightmares revolve around making the spots, as a phantom Gary says, "If you can't have the revolution, you may as well have the breakfast room." In the episode, Gary criticizes Michael for being in advertising—selling things to people who don't need them. Michael defends himself by saying they do *pro bono* work as well, but Elliot is cynical about this. Thus Michael mediates between Gary's and Elliot's values. He does as Elliot does but with guilt, praising his infant daughter for "not giving a damn about money—and if daddy were smart he'd have the same attitude."

The centerpiece of the episode occurs midway through in the form of a fantasy Michael has about facing a tribunal of his peers. The charge? Being a yuppie. While waiting on the soundstage, Michael imagines that he has been abducted by terrorists and brought before a tribunal in an abstract setting reminiscent of the futuristic blued-out day-for-night look featured in the Network 23 boardroom sequences in *Max Headroom*. After charging him with "ideological corruption and decadent materialism," Gary calls Michael a "profit-mongering capitalist." In an amazingly Brechtian sequence in which all the characters (including Elliot) are dressed as 1960s radicals wearing headbands and raising their fists in a "power to the people" salute, Michael is placed on trial. The sequence parodies the Marxist lingo of student radicalism, as when Gary proclaims, "This man is clearly a dupe of the materialist yuppie elite, blindly aping the current fashions of the decadent ruling class." Gary leads the charge, as the incompetent secretary accuses Michael of being "heartless and cruel" (of course job competency was not a hippie value).

> *Elliot*: I object. This man is merely a dupe of the imperialist yuppie elite. I mean he didn't intend to . . . [something house]. He had a momentary lapse of ideological judgment.
> *Michael (screaming)*: The house doesn't work. It's a wreck.
> *Elliot*: And he admits his crime of using consumerist propaganda to sell hundreds of useless objects to unsuspecting members of the downtrodden proletariat.
> *Michael*: Wait a second. You were there. You helped start the com-

pany. I wanted to be a writer. I didn't want to go into advertising, I just couldn't make a living, you understand.

Gary: Which brings us to his worst transgression. His avaricious rush into the trappings and complacency of monogamous bourgeois family life, his spineless toadying to the acquisitive ways of his new masters and a complete betrayal of his earlier beliefs. Yuppie!

The "mob" begins chanting an accusatory "yuppie yuppie yuppie," all the while shaking their fists in the style of an anti–Vietnam War protest.

Michael, over shots of Janie, Nancy, and others protests: "I am not a yuppie. Yuppies only want new cars and CDs. I want those things too, but I can't afford them. Doesn't that count?"

Gary calls for a verdict. Amidst the crowd chanting "guilty, guilty," Hope looks up and pronounces the sentence "guilty." Michael weeps as the mob disperses, chanting what appears to be a combination of "yuppie" and "guilty" (the words *do* sound alike). On an extreme close-up, we return to Michael's "reality," sitting on the soundstage where they will shoot the ad.

Thus in the third episode, the writers of *thirtysomething* anticipated every charge that would ever be made against them. Yet the positioning of the yuppie tribunal fantasy is complex. First of all, it is subjective from Michael's point of view, enabling it to be read as, on the one hand, just another example of Michael's "whining" and, on the other hand, as a kind of artistic summing up of the existential dilemma of 1980s baby boomers. As I will argue in the next chapter, Brechtian modernism has become an art discourse accessible to the upscale TV audience rather than a radically transgressive break with the notion of art. In addition, everyone except Michael is part of the hippie mob, so it is easy to turn the fantasy against him while redeeming the other thirtysomethings. But why should Michael be less a yuppie than Hope or the others? The show defines him as such in order to focus the negative implications of the yup word on the character you love to hate. Yet a more materialist analysis would reveal Hope to be every bit as complicit in yuppie values as Michael, as she betrays feminism in order to have babies and depend on a man. Clearly *thirtysomething* is not interested in materialism; it prefers to treat yuppiedom as a spiritual crisis.

In the fantasy Michael defends his life against the yup word and the remainder of the program bears out his self-defense. The next scene returns us to the reality of the kitchen where Ellen has to walk through a plastic sheet to discuss the young hunk with Hope. When Michael enters, he and Ellen spar over his "power suit" and her shoulder pads. As Michael whines to Hope about his loss of self, she embraces him in a configuration in which Michael occupies one arm and Janie the other, while Ellen provides an ironic commentary.

Then, in another blued-out dream sequence, Michael discusses life with his immigrant Jewish grandfather. "A man gets on with his life. That's what he does," his grandfather tells him. Zayda tells him to quit protesting and go get a haircut. The dream ends with organ chords. As if fueled by this advice, at the Michael and Elliot Company office, Michael decisively takes the dishonest job and tries to fire the incompetent secretary, but at the last minute he wimps out on the latter (many episodes later, she will quit on them).

At home, Hope discusses the house and family with the young hunk while making coffee in a Krups automatic pot. The newly decisive Michael returns home to fire the carpenter-hunk . He prefers to leave the kitchen unfinished rather than the way it is going to look. As an exhausted Michael conks out in bed, Hope yells at him: "You're upset because your business is doing well and you have to rent a space so you can film a commercial. You're upset because you're spending a lot of money which you earned on a house which you love so you can fix it up in certain way and have a big party so you can show it off. What is it about you that makes it impossible for you to enjoy the things you have?" At this point yuppie guilt is transformed into good, old-fashioned Jewish guilt and thus absolved through the intervention of the saintly Hope. As if to celebrate this resolution of guilt, we see the preparation for the housewarming party done in slapstick sped-up motion. At the party, Gary and Michael debate whether Gary really ever did anything political in college and Jerry Stahl (the man Hope had an affair with eight years ago) shows up. He's a nerd. But things take another twist when the episode ends on a utopian moment that is not as easily readable as the absolution for materialism.

After the official party—to the music of Joni Mitchell's "Circle Game"—the friends form their own circle on the Steadmans' living-room floor. "There'll be new dreams maybe better dreams," Joni sings, as the community of friends grooves to the song. Fade out on the blissful couple with child surrounded by friends in a romantic haze. In this utopian moment, a charge Gary leveled against Michael in the fantasy sequence that has not been addressed thus far in the narrative is now taken up: his avaricious rush into the trappings and complacency of monogamous bourgeois family life. But here it is possible to see that the tribalism of the Steadman clan can yield a more utopian reading of the conclusion to the episode. Whatever kind of family the thirty-somethings constitute, it is not exactly isolated and nuclear. Or rather, it *is* a nuclear family consisting of a patriarch (Michael), a Madonna (Hope), and a set of overgrown children (Melissa, Gary, Elliot, Ellen, and sometimes Nancy).

This reconfiguration of the family is brought out in a fantasy Hope has in episode 6, broadcast on 13 November 1987 and dealing with the gathering of the clan for Thanksgiving. Hope sees all the others in Janie's crib dressed as infants, throwing tantrums and shouting "mommy" at her. In another fantasy sequence, a feverish Hope imagines she is dead and looks at ghosts of future Thanksgivings (a combination of Ebenezer Scrooge and *It's a Wonderful Life*). The episode once again concludes with the entire "family" eating in bed together on Thanksgiving. There is a cut to a group photo in Hope's album. The album closes . . . the end. Once again, the clan unites in a moment that reverses the entire trajectory of the episode. Hope had refused to play mommy at Thanksgiving in favor of a quiet weekend spent sorting through her photo albums. In the end, these goals prove to be mutually obtainable. For this was not your mother's Thanksgiving dinner; rather it was a six-ties-inspired tribal dream of a new kind of family constituted by a circle of friends. This utopian reconfiguration of the nuclear family around a chosen family has been a part of the yuppie dream at least since *The Big Chill.* And although the dream is tainted—in both cases the tribe couldn't gather without the actual nuclear family at its center—it gives us an alternative to the Reagan era's glorification of the traditional nuclear family that can be read as progressive by baby boomers.

If the Steadmans' 1987 Thanksgiving is a tribal affair, however, the Christmas that follows is rather more ambiguous about reconstituting the nuclear family. The episode is threaded through with references to pregnancy and babies, as Michael and Elliot take on an ad campaign for pregnant aerobics (another mockery of yuppie culture). Conflict arises between Michael and Melissa when her photos of the exercising moms-to-be prove to be too "arty." Subsequently, a major rift between the Jewish cousins occurs over Melissa's relationship with a famous photographer.

Gary suggests that Michael is jealous of Melissa because she's an artiste and he's a hack. This is a common theme of the show: the failed artist who turns to commercial work, the novelist who becomes an account executive, the photographer who does brochures, the sellout and the cop-out. It is no coincidence that TV writer/producers would invoke such a theme when given an opportunity to produce a show about their own lives. After all, if Scott Fitzgerald could produce narratives of selling out to the screen trade, why not Marshall Herskovitz and Edward Zwick? In *thirtysomething*, however, the selling out of art seems to be linked to the yuppie sellout of 1960s antimaterialist values, as in Michael's fantasy sequence in episode 3. Another use of a Joni Mitchell song over leads into Michael's flashbacks of him and Melissa, as she urges him to become a writer instead of going to business school. Not coincidentally, Melissa and Gary (and later Susannah) are the only characters to retain 1960s values into the eighties.

The dispute is resolved at the end of the episode when Michael comes home to discover Hope holding Janie, a Madonna with Child in matching black velvet dresses with white lace collars, lighting the Hanukkah candles. He is moved to tears when he realizes that Melissa gave them the menorah. He and Melissa embrace to the strains of Joni Mitchell (It's coming on Christmas, they're cutting down the trees / They're putting up reindeers and singing songs of joy and peace / Oh I wish I had a river I could skate away on), a kind of baby boomer's anti-Christmas carol; then as the music continues, the scene holds on a tableau of the entire Steadman family embracing. It is not entirely clear from the Christmas episode that *thirtysomething* has endorsed the conventional nuclear family. Yet when the glance/object shot of Michael coming in on Hope and Janie is transferred to the second season credits and repeated every week, that is the effect. The use of these two shots in the credits anchors their meaning in a permanent tableau of nuclear family unity.

Yuppie culture as explored by *thirtysomething* is thus deeply contradictory. From this point, the yuppie thematics of the show move away from the tribal family to focus on the character of Gary, the Beowulf scholar, as the less than exemplary contrast to Michael Steadman. The episode immediately following Christmas explores Gary's inability to form a lasting relationship with a woman. Both Melissa and Gary have to have Michael and Hope's approval of their prospective partners, giving them a kind of adolescent status—and remember, these are the characters most unconventional politically; to be a leftist/hippie in the 1980s is to be infantile. In fact, Gary is defined by his antimaterialist values in combination with a retrograde attitude toward women—the profile of the macho 1960s radical male. This balancing act between Michael and Gary finds Gary coming out on top in political correctness with Michael ahead on sensitivity and responsibility to women (the second-wave yuppie's version of feminism).

77 Yuppie Envy and Yuppie Guilt

Yet Gary's immature treatment of Melissa and others reflects negatively on his politics as well. This strand comes under pressure in the episode (about the twentieth of the first season) in which Gary finds out he's been denied tenure while Ellen applies for a mortgage. The program opens with Hope and Ellen discussing Ellen's buying her apartment, while Gary discusses tenure with Michael and Melissa. It is as if these were two entirely contrasting spheres—high finance and academics. But we soon learn they are not, as Gary fantasizes his tenure battle as a medieval epic. The parallel editing of the Ellen and Gary plots makes a point: Ellen compares the loss of values in her career as an urban administrator to Gary's disillusionment with academic politics. The moral is that Gary doesn't understand how to work in institutions; his warmed-over sixties humanitarian values are a symptom of his emotional immaturity. It turns out that a knowledge of *demographics* is what separates Michael from Gary; that's why Gary can't switch over to advertising, according to Michael. Gary is also contrasted with the younger pre-med and graduate students who deal in "politics," whereas he deals in the "intrinsic quality" of work. Thus Gary is shown to be less mature and realistic than the generation behind him as well. As in other episodes, the contrast between Michael and Gary is one of image as well as values, or rather one could say that the two project different fashion statements. Michael wears a trendy suit and tie matching combo, Gary old academic lefty clothes. In marketing terms, the choice is between a Michael or a Gary outfit; in fact, the catalog of clothing based on the show allows you to choose either one. Putting aside for the moment the writers' astonishing lack of research into tenure procedures in English departments, it is clear that the purpose of the episode is to break down an earlier binary opposition in which Gary represents idealism, Michael maturity and compromise. In the episode's narrative resolution, Michael accuses Gary of being self-destructive, but when Gary accepts this diagnosis, Michael backs off. At the end, when Gary grovels to his departmental mentor, there is a sense of regret and lost idealism, yet the moral is that a man has to play by the rules. We all have to grow up, have children, buy condos, and curry favor at work.

The tenure episode ends, but Gary's path to "maturity" becomes a continuing story line. In the episode where he meets Susannah, Gary fails at a liberal attempt to counsel a black teenager who turns out to have higher sᴀᴛ scores than Gary had. Gary and Melissa discuss having a baby. In the end Gary is able to bond with the teenager on the basis of his immaturity and failed career—the kid feels sorry for him.

The "Gary" Jacket

We had the original Gary Jacket just hanging in our office. It was to be the prototype reference sample for all future production.

Gary of course was, sadly, gone forever. He'd have no further use for it. Then, a few months ago we learned that Peter Horton was looking for the jacket and asking around about it.

Why? We couldn't understand. The sleeves were smudged and dirty. Elbows started to fray. Threads loosening. Why would anyone want it? Could it be that Peter had an emotional attachment to the jacket? He wasn't told we had it.

Soon thereafter, a **thirty**something fashion show was held in a ballroom at the N.Y. Hilton. Melanie Mayron (Melissa), Polly Draper (Ellyn), and Peter Horton all flew in from California. Their supportive attendance was so welcomed. At the end of the runway presentation we presented flowers to our lady celebrity visitors, Melanie and Polly. And to Peter—The Gary Jacket.

Need we tell you the boyishly gleeful smile that crossed his face? Peter hung around for about another hour—graciously chatting and signing autographs. All the time holding tightly to the jacket under one arm. Never once did he put it down....It was then we understood.

The jacket is being reproduced now—exactly. Even the "Knights" on the back. Everything. Except the embroidered name. If you want your name instead of Gary, just let us know. No extra charge. But please allow an extra month delivery.

U-374 — Unisex – (also see p.47)
Green/White S/M/L/XL – $179

*370— 100% Sandwashed Silk
– Quilted Jacket –
Olive – S/M/L – $79*

Ultimately, the political contrast between Gary and Michael gets played out early in the second season in the first full episode (broadcast 17 January 1989) since episode 3 to deal explicitly with yuppie political guilt. Michael and Elliot take on an advertising campaign for an old campus radical pal, now a yuppie managing the campaign of a not very politically correct female candidate. The political campaign sends Michael into flashbacks of campus protests in which Michael and Gary appear as longhairs, and their political contact (Jerry Kravitz) makes a fiery New Left speech while occupying a campus building. These memories are "first wave" baby boomer memories; as always when the theme of yuppie guilt reappears, the *Big Chill* thematics take over. Gary tells Michael that Kravitz's candidate is "slime." Michael agrees but says, "I keep forgetting that college and reality are incompatible." This is the first time since episode 3 that an entire show has focused on yuppie political guilt and the loss of social consciousness since the sixties. Is it a coincidence that the air date of the episode also marks the end of the Reagan presidency?

Politics returns to *thirtysomething* with the introduction of Susannah, whose role is to evoke yuppie guilt in everybody else and yet to be always the social and emotional misfit. She is without friends and family—the values most stressed by the extended cast family of the series. The big set piece of the 17 January episode occurs when Gary brings Susannah to dinner at Hope and Michael's. The others are embarrassed because Susannah smokes and doesn't eat meat. She's appalled by their cavalier attitudes toward politics. When the group describes a country vacation they are going to take together, they do so in terms of characters from *The Big Chill* ("it's very *Big Chill*"). (This is the only explicit reference to *The Big Chill* in the entire series.) The strained dinner conversation pits Michael against Susannah in a battle over yuppie values. The two squabble about the need for private investment versus the effect of displaced people. He's taking the Reaganite position: "Gentrification—it's a horrible word but unfortunately it's part of the natural life cycle of the city." When Gary and Susannah leave, Ellen remarks on her coldness; in a parallel conversation, Susannah tells Gary, "It's all very nice if you know the secret handshake." Rapid parallel intercut scenes alternate their reactions to Susannah and hers to them. All are negative and judgmental. An extended debate ensues over Michael's involvement in the campaign. Michael's claim is that he is *responsible* for family, employees, and friends. He gives long speeches about the bottom line, being cautious like his father, and "next time we'll be more vigilant." This is a real thesis play in which political purity is played off against patriarchal responsibility (and "friendship and loyalty"), and the latter comes out ahead. Gary and Susannah emerge as the perfect couple of the Bush era: Gary has no politics; she has no friends or feelings. Clearly the latter is a greater deficit.

The political emphasis of the program appears to shift at the end of the Reagan presidency. As Bush takes office, Michael and Elliot lose their business; the focus shifts from fear of success to fear of failure; Michael drops his ambivalence and starts to climb the corporate ladder. Miles Drentell becomes a central character. Yet as this shift occurs, we are given a glimpse of the past in an arty episode that traces Michael's history with Elliot. Flashbacks reveal Michael as having been "quixotic," that is, idealistic—his boss says to save his quixotic impulses for his fiction. The flashback diegesis merges with the present as the younger Michael and Elliot enter the office that the present Michael and Elliot are packing up. The only really intense homosocial moment between Michael and Elliot occurs in this doubled space when they are first going into business together and Michael suddenly thanks Elliot for making him take risks. This touching moment seems to bring to a close the *Big Chill* thematics of the first two seasons. The nostalgia and generational awareness that permeates many of the early episodes will be displaced in the seasons that ensue. As Elliot remarked in a first season episode, "By the time Mozart was my age, he had composed *The Magic Flute* and managed to be dead for a year." Did this overachievement make Mozart a yuppie?

It is no coincidence that two academic/feminist commentaries on *thirtysomething* refer to the show as "postmodern" (Torres 1989; Probyn 1990). What is postmodern about *thirtysomething* is its knowing cynicism about values the characters nevertheless embrace. Rather than being an exception to the yuppie sensibility, this complicit critique defines the yuppie sensibility. It unites into a common cultural moment such diverse phenomena as *thirtysomething, Metropolitan Home, The Yuppie Handbook,* and academic postmodern theory. And yet in the act of discussing the show's postmodernity, both critics reference a kind of intertextuality that is resolutely modernist. For yuppie TV was more than just a marketing strategy; it was a significant aesthetic development of Reagan-era television.

Notes

1 Analysis in this section is based on all episodes of *L.A. Law* in the first two seasons (1986–1987, 1987–1988) and the fall 1988 episodes beginning just before the November election.

2 This discussion is based on a careful study of tapes of every episode up to "New Baby" in 1989.

4

Art Discourse in 1980s Television:

Modernism as Postmodernism

Since television was not originally conceptualized as an art form at all, TV programs needed to be constructed as artistic artifacts. This was the function of "art discourses" around yuppie television in the 1980s. By "art discourse" I mean that the definition of what is artistic is determined discursively: it is culturally constructed by social groups who have the power to define aesthetic value for their times. However, these cultural gatekeepers do not themselves define art so relativistically. Thus an art discourse at any given time will always have both an economic or power component, that is, a sociological part; and a formal or artistic component, that is, an aesthetic part. Arguably, then, the moment American network television was figured discursively as art occurred when *thirtysomething* was taken up by the yuppie press and its scripts were published in the form of a book (see below). An even more pointed moment occurred with the discourses surrounding *Twin Peaks* (1990–1991), a moment that falls outside the time span of my discussion but not, I believe, outside the scope of my analysis.

I would argue that during the 1980s, the hallmark of artistic expression within the narrative arts meant something different for the educated middle classes than it did for the more specialized academic critical community. If in the 1930s Brechtian modernism was the peak of art discourse in the theater world, and if in the 1960s Brechtian art cinema was the peak of art discourse among film cognoscenti, then in the 1980s Brechtian modernism at last became art discourse among the educated elite who produced and (less frequently) viewed American network television. In short, by the time certain formalist notions of modernism were rendered passé in academic art discourse, these same ideas were just coming into vogue for the yuppie audience of American network television.

Cinematic Precedents: TV as Cinema

The cinematic itself now lays claim to prestige. No matter how great his or her TV work or how inferior his (and rarely her) films (e.g., James Brooks: *The Mary Tyler Moore Show* vs. *Terms of Endearment)*, the term "TV artist" remains a logical impossibility. As late as the 1980s for the educated middle class, a bad Fellini movie (a redundancy to be sure) could qualify as art; a great sitcom or a daytime soap, never. In fact, the clearest indicator of *thirtysomething*'s art status came when critics and coworkers started to claim that *thirtysomething* was not television at all: it was cinema. *Los Angeles Times* TV critic Howard Rosenberg said of cocreators Marshall Herskovitz and Ed Zwick, "These are filmmakers making a pit stop" (1988). *New York* magazine quotes film director Claudia Weill, "It's very unusual television. Ed and Marshall encourage you to turn every episode into a little movie" (Hoban 1988, p. 51). And *American Film*, the publication of the American Film Institute, echoes, "It's shot more like a film than a weekly drama" (Lantos 1987, p. 51).

A number of cinematic developments prepared the way for *thirtysomething*'s acceptance as art by the yuppie spectator. A crucial precedent was the emergence of Woody Allen for the title of America's greatest director by the art house crowd and the unusually wide distribution of his films. At first considered a comic genius as an entertainer, Allen emerged as a film artist with his modernist, formalist works of the late seventies, *Annie Hall* (1977) and *Manhattan* (1979). But it was during the eighties that Woody Allen was enshrined as an *artiste* by such gatekeepers as high-end trade book and academic book publishers.[1] From the mid-eighties until 1993, Woody Allen, filmmaker, has been subjected to the entire gamut of critical methodologies from Coleridgeian notions of organicism to poststructuralism.

For example, in *The Films of Woody Allen*, Sam B. Girgus argues that "because he is a celebrity and part of a world of mass entertainment, Allen's true artistic achievement and significance are easily minimized. This is unfortunate because Allen's work should be studied with the same close attention given to other serious artists and writers. While books about Allen and his work have accumulated steadily over the years, few detailed studies of the artistry of the individual films have appeared" (Girgus 1993, p. 59). Several of these books on Woody Allen speak of his growth and development from film to film in language derived from Romantic literary aesthetics: "Accordingly, the innovative visualization and imaginative dramatization of narrative desire in

Annie Hall achieves even greater visual and literary complexity and originality in *Manhattan*"; and "*Zelig* is a masterpiece of originality and the film that should convince any remaining doubters that Woody Allen is, unquestionably, a genius" (Spignesi 1992, p. 180).

Woody Allen is repeatedly cited in these critical works as the director who brings twentieth-century modernism to American cinema. In this regard, cinematic modernism comes to TV brought to you by a modernist tradition that is distinctly counter to classic Hollywood cinema, as detailed at length by Thomas Schatz in a discussion of "Modernist Strategies in the New Hollywood" (1983, p. 232). Schatz's charting of the distinctions between classical and modernist strategies in new Hollywood cinema is derived from a similar set of oppositions Peter Wollen set up in his widely influential 1970s discussion of Jean-Luc Godard's modernism which in turn was derived from Bertolt Brecht's even more influential 1930 essay "The Modern Theater Is the Epic Theater" (1979, originally 1930, p. 37). In each case, a column of characteristics of either classical Hollywood narrative or in Brecht's case "dramatic theater" is opposed to another column of the countercharacteristics of modernist cinema, the avant-garde, or, as originally for Brecht, his "epic theater," whose impact on theorizing cinematic modernism in general and Godard in particular has been so profound. In each case, the old-fashioned, reactionary side of the model is a kind of dramatic unity that leads to viewer fascination and identification that the authors see as politically retrograde. The modernist side then is seen as using specific techniques that run counter to the creation of identification and thus "jolt" the viewer into a realization of the politically complicit character of the classical tradition involved, whether cinematic or theatrical. In each case the modernist techniques are dependent functions of the classical ones, to use Wollen's term a "countercinema." The modernist paradigm renders self-conscious the invisible power of the classical dramatic structure in which the viewer becomes an intoxicated subject rather than a critical intellectual.

Schatz cites *Annie Hall* as a film that "virtually demands that the viewer adopt a modernist perspective, a self-conscious attitude toward Allen and his narrative." And yet, as Schatz insightfully goes on to note, *Annie Hall* is not an "inaccessible" film: "So while *Annie Hall* represents one of the more extreme examples of modernist technique in a popular Hollywood movie, the audience's general familiarity with Woody Allen's persona and the logic of the standup comedy routine tempers that modernism and renders it easily accessible to the majority of viewers" (Schatz 1983, pp. 225–231). Substitute the audience's familiarity with soap opera and the logic of the family melodrama, and Schatz could be writing about *thirtysomething*.

In other words, the vein of modernism that would impact on 1980s yuppie TV was not the overtly self-reflexive and intertextual developments of *Stardust Memories* (1980), *Zelig* (1983), and *Purple Rose of Cairo* (1985), films that are primarily interested, as was Godard, in deconstructing the language of cinema, but rather the "warm and fuzzy" modernism of *Annie Hall* and *Manhattan,* which blended modernistic techniques derived from the Felliniesque-Brechtian-Godardian tradition with the angst of contemporary yuppie-couple relationships derived from Ingmar Bergman.

The work of the quintessential European art cinema director Ingmar Bergman had been broadcast on PBS in the form of the serial drama *Scenes from a Marriage,* a title that might have applied equally well to *thirtysomething.* If Woody Allen movies captured the feel of Manhattan early yuppie culture, then the Bergman serial influenced the heavily dramatic emphasis on relationships that was the other side to *thirtysomething*'s quick wit. In fact, it was commonly acknowledged that Bergman had been a distinct influence on the "serious" Woody Allen films beginning with *Interiors* (1978). And the intertextual connections between Fellini's *8½* and Woody Allen's *Stardust Memories*[2] remain a much-analyzed component of the history of the self-reflexive art movie tradition of the portrait of the film director as the Romantic artist, a tradition that would find its way into *thirtysomething* via Michael's and Elliot's positions as "creative" advertisers. The Fellini-Bergman connection redoubled the significance of the prestige of European art cinema for commercial artists wanting to lay claim to being "serious" artists, i.e., Woody Allen, James Brooks, Edward Zwick, and Marshall Herskovitz. Brecht/Bergman/Fellini/Godard/Woody Allen/*thirtysomething*—this is the trajectory I am positing for *thirtysomething*'s introduction of early twentieth-century modernism to mid-eighties television.

The self-reflexive and modernist techniques cited by critics of *Annie Hall* and *Manhattan* become the "antirealist" devices that Sasha Torres has noted as the opposite side to *thirtysomething*'s oft-noted realism: "*thirtysomething* often includes explicitly anti-realist moments . . . which depict dreams or fantasies in ways that disrupt realist representational conventions" (1989, p. 89). But just how disruptive of realist representational conventions are dream sequences in 1987? Representations of fantasies have permeated audiovisual entertainment forms at least as far back as the classic Hollywood musicals of the 1930s to 1950s.

They are central to television's representational conventions as well. Indeed a common type of fantasy transition that has become a standard part of the language of daytime soap opera may be even more disruptive than many of the fantasy techniques *thirtysomething* employs. In the daytime version, a scene that would represent the ultimate fulfillment of a character's wish is shown to the viewers as a realist representation. Only at the end of the sequence are we let in to the secret that this idyllic moment has been the dream of a character in the primary narrative. The regular viewer, however, is clued in by the improbability of the event taking place in the dream to the actual narrative (usually the dream depicts an unlikely confession of love). This technique is disruptive because it leaves the viewer suspended between the pleasurable fulfillment of the dream's desire and a sense of the uncanny: this can't be happening. The moment of returning to "reality" is thus always something of a jolt and something of a disappointment. Daytime soaps employ more obviously cued fantasies as well: dreams marked off by dissolves or cameo effects, and ones full of fantasy in their mise-en-scène, as when a romantic couple dances cheek to cheek in Fred and Ginger costumes.

Although such fantasies are "antirealist" in a formal sense, they are not supposed to disrupt our immersion in the serial's narrative to the extent that "multiple diegesis" does in the films of Jean-Luc Godard. Godard will insert characters from history reading political tracts into a seemingly conventional narrative: the degree of narrative disruption is presumed to be much greater because eventually the primary narrative gets absorbed into its interruptions. On the other hand, by the time we get to television, the influence of the Brechtian tradition from modernist art cinema is hard to separate from the influence of our more native entertainment traditions. That is to say, the distinction between "dream sequences" and "multiple diegesis" becomes difficult to make in practice. To paraphrase Schatz, *thirtysomething* is not inaccessible. Nor is inaccessibility necessarily viewed as a worthy goal for postmodern art.

thirtysomething's antirealism falls somewhere in between these two extremes (dream sequences and multiple diegeses) that are yet not oppositions. In many cases, the fantasies are simply wish fulfillments in the manner of fantasies in daytime soaps or musicals. In the fifth episode of the first season, for example, Hope is jealous of Melissa's freedom. Her daughter Janie, in a technique borrowed from the film *Look Who's Talking,* gives her a lecture: "Mom, you want a Saturday night." We segue to a blue-filtered romantic dance fantasy of Hope and

Michael with Michael Feinstein at the grand piano crooning standards by Gershwin and company. Throughout the episode, vignettes from the lives of the thirtysomethings are interspersed with musical interludes of Feinstein singing love songs against a backdrop of midnight blue. Not only does this mimic the alternation of levels of reality and fantasy between narrative segments and musical numbers in classic Hollywood musicals, it also imitates some of the daytime soap opera fantasy sequences based on these musicals. The setting up of a reality/fantasy, drab/perfect duality aligns *thirtysomething* with the most venerable of show business traditions for the use of "antirealism" expressed as fantasy.[3]

Many of the antirealist moments in *thirtysomething* follow out this pattern. In the first season Thanksgiving episode, Hope imagines scenes from her photo album come to life. As the camera pans left, the youthful image of Hope and Ellen addresses a similar snapshot of Michael and Gary. Although this sequence does involve a manipulation across space and time, its wit places it in an entertainment as well as a Godardian tradition. Later, Hope imagines all the others in a crib dressed as infants, throwing tantrums and shouting "mommy" at her, in a typical use of fantasy as nightmarish wish fulfillment. In a fantasy sequence from the same episode, a feverish Hope imagines she's dead and looks at ghosts of future Thanksgivings, echoing the classical Hollywood film most often quoted in TV drama—*It's a Wonderful Life.*[4] Other fantasies appear to imitate the mythic strain of fantasy materials in children's fairy tales, films, and musicals: Gary imagines his tenure battle as a medieval epic; the children's story that Nancy is telling to Ethan comes to life for the viewer as well. Is this disruptive of realist conventions? It depends on how much and which TV you watch, how well you tolerate musicals, and if you know Godard does stuff like that and he is supposed to be subversive.

When TV does employ multiple diegeses, the intertextual references tend to be to other media sources. For *thirtysomething,* this means non-quality and tabloid television such as the Home Shopping Channel, game shows, and *Lifestyles of the Rich and Famous,* all of which are referenced in the show. For example, Melissa imagines herself on a comedic game show called "Beat the Biological Clock." In a humorous fantasy sequence with Robin Leach, the "worst parents of the year award" goes to the Steadmans. After Ellen fires him from a job promoting the city, Michael goes home and becomes addicted to the Home Shopping Channel; as a result of viewing daytime TV, he decides to quit advertising. *thirtysomething*'s baby boomers' dystopic fantasies, in other words, are not science fiction but rather visions of their lives as schlocky daytime TV shows.

Usually, the use of fantasy material is intermittent; on occasion, entire episodes are structured around different levels of reality—these tend to be the episodes considered "arty" and the ones included in the published collection of scripts (discussed below). These are the episodes most typical of the modernist manipulation of time and narrative: even the episode ("New Baby") in which Gary and Susannah's baby is born fits under this rubric owing to its clever use of reverse time punctuated by a ticking clock. Sometimes the writers of *thirtysomething* nod to a source in the mainstream tradition of art cinema, as in the "Rashomon" episode from the first season, in which a fight between Nancy and Elliot is depicted from multiple points of view, thus involving a multiple-perspective repetition of story events reminiscent of the famous Japanese film. In another art-cinema episode, Melissa's grandmother (Sylvia Sidney) has flashbacks to her ghetto childhood. Elaine (Melissa's mother, played by Phyllis Newman) also has flashbacks to her childhood in the dress shop. When Melissa rejects her offer to inherit the family dress shop, the matriarch (Rose) has a flashback to her mother's death in the old country.

Other episodes make intertextual references to the pantheon of directors of American cinema. In the Dana Delaney guest-starring episode from the first season, Gary is watching *North by Northwest* on TV. He goes into a fantasy black-and-white cinema sequence in which he imagines himself and Elliot in a version of *Strangers on a Train* and Melissa in *Rear Window*. In the Hitchcock sequences everyone psychoanalyzes Gary's inability to commit to a relationship with a woman, a pointed reference to the thematics of *North by Northwest.*

Of the "art cinema" episodes of *thirtysomething*, two stand out in their quasi-Brechtian use of multiple diegeses. Broadcast in December during the delayed TV season of fall 1988–spring 1989 with only three new episodes to be shown in the 1988 portion of that TV season, the premiere episode and the second season Christmas show seem distinctive as small experimental "movies." The season premiere features a secondary diegesis in which Hope finds and relives the diary of a woman named Sally who lived in her house during World War II. Although the daytime soap opera *Days of Our Lives* would feature a Civil War diary diegesis for its May 1989 sweeps, *thirtysomething* gave the flashbacks an aura of art cinema. The Christmas show—titled "The Mike van Dyke Show" and reprinted in the collection of scripts—takes the media-referencing Brechtian strain as far as the show ever went with it.

The diary episode juxtaposes fantasies of marriage and family based on old World War II movies with Hope and Michael's decision to have more children. In a seeming subplot, Hope does a radon test in the basement of the Steadmans' domicile; later this is linked to the main theme: the tenuousness of the bonds of family life. The episode is based on nostalgia around the restoration of old-fashioned family life; this is signified visually by the sepia-toned antique quality of the cinematography in the World War II sequences. The episode is full of yuppie angst. Elliot tells Michael that he and Nancy made a prenuptial agreement that she would have two children and cater to his every need and he would systematically destroy her confidence and self-esteem. Hope compares her career and the radon test to the World War II woman's losing her baby and with Sally's husband's being missing in action—we have no more control over things than they do, she tells Michael. In the final segment of the program, diegeses merge—Sally addresses Hope; she tells Hope, "Take care of the garden; it's yours now." This is a Godardian moment in that historical personages address characters in the present, but it is one imbued with tremendous sentimentality—family not politics. It represents the erasure of the forces of history and of generations, not their juxtaposition. At the end, Hope and Michael reconcile in Sally's garden. The episode ends on a lingering shot of the house as Hope continues writing the diary. It is implied that, despite Hope's reservations, she and Michael will have another child, an implication that is confirmed in the next (Christmas 1988) episode.

The diary episode takes the Bergmanesque strain of the show to a nostalgic extreme. More than any other episode, this one tempts me to offer a reading of it as deeply reactionary and antifeminist. And yet one could argue that it depicts the "reality" of family life for the baby boom generation as opposed to the World War II generation, whose lack of choices made life simpler. Oddly enough, despite its artiness, the episode serves the same ideological function that the Civil War diary story line did for the audience of *Days of Our Lives*: it models the relationship of a contemporary couple around nostalgia for a heroic past.

"The Mike van Dyke Show"

Perhaps the best-known episode of *thirtysomething*, "The Mike van Dyke Show" also deals in dual diegeses, but this time the nostalgia is for the stable marriages of sixties sitcoms rather than for sepia-toned war movies. And yet, there is still a juxtaposition of a "contemporary" reality with one that is historical and is visually signaled as such—in this case, via the use of black-and-white TV images that serve the same function as sepia did in the previous episode. Since these were two of the three episodes broadcast in the fall 1988 season, one would expect them to have strong narrative continuity, but aside from the thread of Hope's second pregnancy, debated in the diary episode and realized as a miraculous act of God in "The Mike van Dyke Show," the links are purely thematic and structural.

Scripted by cocreators Zwick and Herskovitz, "The Mike van Dyke Show" was the second Christmas episode written for *thirtysomething*'s unconventional TV families. As the cowriters explained it in their published introduction to the script:

> In our first season, we'd been pretty happy about our Christmas show. Richard had managed to evoke many of our mixed feelings about mixed marriages. We were all proud of what had to have been the only consciously ambivalent holiday show on network television. . . . We had also wanted to talk about TV itself—how its shopworn constructs had taught us, for better or worse, a way of seeing the world. How we, as writers had somehow bought its portrayal of an emotional landscape absent of contradictions and ambivalences, where people always say exactly what they mean, where problems are nicely shaped and tidily resolved. And why, in trying to do a show whose self-conscious mandate was to only tell the "truth," were we always coming back to the familiar rhythms of "Hi, honey, I'm home"?

Zwick and Herskovitz go on to explain that since *Moonlighting* had already "done" *The Honeymooners*, they would seize for their intertext "a TV show written by writers about writers writing a TV show" (*thirtysomething* Writers 1991, pp. 101–104).

As the episode opens, the *thirtysomething* family is playing Trivial Pursuit while discussing the *Dick van Dyke Show.*[5] As usual, Gary assumes the role of modernist intellectual when he finds himself landing on "television" ("Can't our generation define itself any other way besides what tunes it remembers from old TV shows?"). This leads to a Trivial Pursuit question involving the *Dick van Dyke Show,* about which the thirtysomethings show a deep knowledge. Although the episode rapidly shifts its emphasis to the subject of Christmas, the image of this sixties sitcom has been established as the one that gave the thirtysomethings their expectations for adult married life.

The episode juxtaposes preparations for Christmas, the unveiling of Michael's father's headstone, Ethan's distress over his parents' separation, and an automobile accident involving Hope and Janie with a secondary diegesis in which the *thirtysomething* characters enact imaginary scenes from phantom *Dick van Dyke Show* episodes, all shown from Michael Steadman's point of view. The Dick van Dyke enactments come to Michael in the course of his spiritual journey toward a renewal of his belief in God via a renewal of Jewish religious practices. At moments of crisis within his "real" life, Michael sees his life reenacted within the diegesis of *The Dick van Dyke Show*. Reversing the 1939 symbolism of *The Wizard of Oz*, the television scenes are in glorious black and white. In the first such appearance, the Steadmans' unmanageable mornings are transformed into the exact mise-en-scène of Rob and Laura Petrie's suburban living room, with Michael as Rob and Hope as a reincarnation of Mary Tyler Moore. Accompanied by loud bursts of canned laughter, Hope and Michael act out an inane sixties sitcom plot joined by their sitcomish friends and neighbors portrayed by Nancy and Elliot. In the next fantasy scene, Michael, exhausted from the twin traumas of his father's unveiling and Hope's accident, lies down in front of the TV clutching one of Janie's teddy bears. Suddenly we are into the "Mike van Dyke Show" diegesis taking place on the small screen. This time we're in Rob Petrie's office, where Michael and Elliot are auditioning Santa Clauses for Ethan's Christmas pageant. Paralleling the main story line, the sitcom Michael is worried about Hope's whereabouts. A Santa in a union suit appears, complaining about the television antennas on the rooftops. After numerous scenes involving Michael's relationship to Judaism, synagogue, and God, we are thrown back into the black-and-white world after a scene with a troubled Ethan in the Michael and Elliot office. Again, a videotape takes us inside the monitor of the dream diegesis, this time with Melissa as Rose Marie. Hope is still missing, and the sitcom friends await her return to the suburban living room as the man in the union suit enters, now in full Santa regalia. After Ethan has been convinced that Santa indeed exists, we fade from the "Mike van Dyke Show" to a scene in which Michael takes Ethan home and they discuss the relative merits of being Jewish, of your father being dead, and of your father being divorced. But now the diegeses start to merge. Michael stops off at the synagogue to encounter a Rabbi Markovitz, who turns out to be Kris Kringle from the "Mike van Dyke Show." When, some scenes later, Hope is missing again, Michael turns on the TV and enters the "Mike van Dyke Show." Much like a typical sitcom Christmas show, everyone overcomes skepticism as to the existence of Santa, Elliot gives Nancy a dishwasher, and Elliot (unbeknownst to him but presumably known to

Santa) gets a Thunderbird with fins, thus cementing his marriage. The scene takes a somber turn and once again mixes diegeses when Santa tells Michael that Hope is never coming back. Michael looks at everyone in horror as his face and body are colorized. He walks past the others, still in black and white, out of frame and into the Steadman kitchen. The resolution to the dilemma of the sitcom takes place in the real world, when Michael discovers that Hope is not dying, she's pregnant. Michael realizes he believes in God and returns to the synagogue to discover that Rabbi Markovitz is a young man who has never heard of the other Rabbi Markovitz. The episode ends with Michael going into the sanctuary, donning a yarmulke, and reciting Kaddish for his father. Presumably, Michael has taken the place of the father. If the diary episode represented a spiritual quest for Hope as a woman of the eighties, then this one renders a similar journey for Michael, and with similar results: the affirmation of traditional spirituality, home, and family for the yuppie generation taking place at the tail end of the Reagan presidency. Both of these fall 1988 episodes take their spiritual journeys into the realm of the mystical and even the supernatural, in this sense anticipating the use of secondary diegeses on *Northern Exposure*. As 1989 arrives, the show will turn away from little art movies and back to the melodrama of Gary and Susannah. But for a brief moment, art cinema had come to television.

Literary Authorship: *thirtysomething stories* (the Book)

Foucault has remarked that only certain texts are considered authored (1979, p. 19). For the college-educated (but not too educated), a text's medium counts. That is to say, a book is automatically more authored than a TV show. It is thus not surprising that the elevation of *thirtysomething* to the level of art discourse should be accompanied by the publication of a select few of its scripts in book form by Pocket Books in a "quality" paperback edition titled *thirtysomething stories*. Authorship is attributed on the jacket to "the writers of *thirtysomething*," who provide introductions and annotations. In this way, the writers of *thirtysomething* are promoted as the "creators" of the show, not, as in contemporary art cinema, the directors. It is the *stories* that constitute art, not their embodiment in TV images. This brings out a notable contrast between the use of the terms "creative" and "creator" in literary criticism and in broadcasting or advertising. When applied to the book, the terms take on connotations of Romantic literary authorship, whereas in TV the term "creator" has more legalistic connotations; after the first

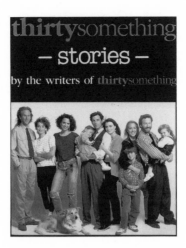

season or even after the first few episodes, the creators are usually not the authors of the scripts. Also, in TV lingo, only Zwick and Herskovitz are the creators; the others are merely writers. To call the writers of the stories "creators" is somewhat ingenuous, given that the book's copyright is held by the MGM/UA television production group. Even more ingenuous is the dedication of the book to the actors whose likenesses appear on the cover: images of writers do not sell books in this arena.

thirtysomething stories does not contain any mention of the broadcast tape dates of the programs or any camera instructions. This makes it seem as if the scripts are being offered as literature rather than television. In addition, the scripts do not give the exact lines that the actors deliver, suggesting that the preexisting script is a more authored and more perfect document than, say, a videotape of the program. This practice also suggests creativity, in that the actors are embroidering the lines or processing them through the characters instead of mouthing the exact words. Even the scripts are not broadcast versions. They show more of the writers' intentions and are more literary. Take, for example, the treatment of yuppiedom in the pilot script. Careful examination reveals discrepancies between the published script and a videotape of the pilot episode along the following lines:

–Ages: The script says Melissa is thirty-two and born in 1956; the broadcast tape says thirty-one and 1960! Despite the implausibility, the effect is that the script makes her older and thus more likely to have been an authentic big chiller/baby boomer.

–The script is more meticulous in drawing out the context of sixties politics now forsaken for yuppiedom, as in the following passage:

> *Elliot*: I know a guy at Penn Savings, like this total freak in high school, I have pictures of him dancing naked at Woodstock. We could blackmail him.
>
> *Michael*: I was supposed to go to Woodstock but I got tonsillitis and my girlfriend decided to go anyway because we were so free and of course she met this other guy and eventually married him, but they're divorced now so I feel better. (*thirtysomething* Writers 1991, p. 26)

This dinner table conversation, fully legible in the script, is obscured in the broadcast text by the overlapping women's conversation about the children spilling milk. Although the women's lines are also given in the script, they follow sequentially from the Woodstock comments without overlapping them.

–The script, in the form of stage directions, makes direct references to yuppie material culture; these are omitted from the final broadcast version:

> THE MOST DELICIOUS MOMENT OF THE DAY: Michael settles into his favorite chair and devotionally holds before him two catalogs, among his life's greatest pleasures: The Sharper Image and the L. L. Bean catalogs . . . as he prepares to plunge into the latest forty-eight-function automatic telephone." (*thirtysomething* Writers 1991, p. 33)

My intent in making these rather biblical scholarly comments on the published scripts versus the videotapes is not to ponder the meaning of the different versions of a canonized text, although it may have that effect. Rather, I wish to point out that the scripts provide a richer literary and analytical context for the cognoscenti among *thirtysomething*'s fans, at the same time elevating what are usually considered erasable video texts to the status of "the book."

On the one hand, then, *thirtysomething stories* constructs the show as art, to be precise, as televisual art marked by the techniques of modernism in theater and cinema. But, *thirtysomething stories*, by placing the actors on the cover in a publicity still, does not reproduce one of the hallmark characteristics of early-twentieth-century modernist art movements: their desire to set themselves in opposition to the mass-produced commercial products of capitalism. That is why the *thirtysomething* phenomenon as a whole may fit under the rubric of modernism, defined as certain formal practices, while not at all conforming to definitions of twentieth-century aesthetic modernism as an historical period in which the goals of art and commerce are opposed ideologically. As Fredric Jameson has argued in "Periodizing the 60s," postmodernism, unlike modernism, is a cultural dominant with a "precise socio-economic functionality." Therefore even if modernism and postmodernism have identical formal features, their meaning differs according to the periodization involved (1988, p. 196). Historically speaking, that is, *thirtysomething* is a *postmodern* phenomenon.

To illustrate this claim, I would like to narrate the ways in which *thirtysomething* was conceptualized as art and commerce at the same time and without any great ideological conflict between the two. In this way, the *thirtysomething* phenomenon can stand as a case study of postmodern *art,* defined as an interwoven whole between a text and its promotional satellites. The challenges this postmodern text poses to the distinction between art and commerce will be taken up in Chapter 6. For now, I would like to look at the circulation of *thirtysomething* from an advertising concept to an aesthetic text and back again.

At the same time *thirtysomething* was being "elevated" to the status of the book, it was being "lowered" to the status of a commodity. But this distinction between high and low culture is itself a modernist one. For *thirtysomething stories,* the book, occupies an ambiguous status as a postmodern cultural phenomenon, on the one hand receiving a favorable review in *Library Journal,* on the other hand being marketed alongside the thirtysomething™ tape cassette soundtrack, the thirtysomething™ baseball cap, and the thirtysomething™ catalog gift certificate in a catalog newsletter sanctioned by the show's producers. As an abstract of an article from *Catalog Age* explains:

> Thirtysomething, a catalog of lifestyle fashions inspired by the television series, is produced by Apparel Resources International Ltd., which has licensed the show's name and logo design from its producer, MGM. The show's cancellation prompted retailers to cancel their orders, but Apparel Resources' president Lenny Heller saw the chance to move the items through mail order. The 24-page catalog's unconventional design depicts the products in off-figure color photos paired with black-and-white lifestyle sketches of the clothing in use. Heller estimates that the catalog will have nearly 25 million names by its third year of business, as a result of the program's upcoming re-introduction through syndication in the spring of 1992. (1992, p. 46)

thirtysomething, as we have seen, emerged out of a demographic category (baby boomers, yuppies) itself based on an imaginary construct of marketing. According to Brad Edmondson, a senior editor of *American Demographics* interviewed in 1988:

> My assessment of *thirtysomething* is that it is a reaction to a demographic phenomenon rather than a cause of anything. . . . My feeling is that marketing trends created *thirtysomething*. I think the creators of the show realized that the median age in this country is creeping up and very deliberately set about turning out a program that would appeal to a very large and very sellable audience. We have studies that show that, in the next decade, the fastest-growing age group will be the thirty-five- to forty-four-year-olds. (Kaplan 1988, p. 80)

Yet Ed Zwick is quoted in the same article as saying "the single attack or criticism of the show that does get to me, that I feel to be unjustified, is the notion that we had at any moment or in any way contrived to target a demographic group—the inception of this, and its growth, was so personal and so organic and so *removed* from any commercial considerations" (Kaplan 1988, p. 85, italics in original). The difference in both language and content between the demographer and the artist is striking.

Within the show, characters were defined by their relationship to advertising, with Hope's goodness being symbolized by consumer advocacy and Michael's increasing corruption by his immersion in the Miles Drentell world of the advertising agency. In addition to the yuppie programs already described, the show would go on to even more scathing critiques of the advertising world; one of the best-known episodes deals with the immorality and dishonesty of advertising. In this 1991 show, Miles Drentell forces Michael to fire the male model in an ad campaign for a right-wing client because the actor was depicted in news footage protesting the Gulf War. Miles symbolizes the corruption of capitalism, while Michael is the Romantic artist, putting his ideals above the demands of capital; Michael is James Joyce, Miles a demonic Steven Spielberg. The episode ends on a moment of high modernist nobility, as Michael quits his job and refuses to come back at Miles's begging. A few episodes later, however, Michael would become Miles Drentell. When *thirtysomething* debuted on Lifetime, this episode was chosen as the personal favorite of the actor who played Miles and was showcased with introductions by that actor.

And yet, at the same time as these episodes were being broadcast, those responsible for the "look" of *thirtysomething* were being hired to make TV commercials that would lend the same aura of realism to Kool Aid and Jif peanut butter. The use of real products on *thirtysomething* (for example, Hope drives a Jeep Cherokee), viewed as an important artistic move toward realism by Marshall Herskovitz, was interpreted by critics of the show as leading to "rampant, gleeful, commercialism" (Kaplan 1988, p. 84).

In addition, plans were being made for commodity tie-ins, including the book of scripts that would signify the show's cultural status. What we have here is a mind-boggling example of art fully penetrated by capital: in its conception, in its execution, and in its consequences. Moreover, *thirtysomething* would have an afterlife in the yuppie's idea of heaven: the direct marketing catalog. If in the stage directions to the scripts Michael's idea of paradise is settling down with the *Sharper Image* catalog, then for the yuppified audience of *thirtysomething*, the show can live on in the form of syndicated reruns while achieving resurrection by itself being transfigured into a direct-mail catalog. To complete the circle, the catalog's initial 25,000 prospects came from space ads in *TV Guide, Us, New York,* and *The Village Voice,* as well as from list rentals from *The Sharper Image* and *The Right Start* (*Catalog Age* 1992, p. 46).

What is interesting about the thirtysomething™ catalog and related cult activities that I am about to describe is their contrast to other significant cults that have formed around canceled TV shows. In the many (excellent) studies of fan cultures surrounding *Star Trek,* for instance, there seems to be general agreement that the original broadcast of *Star Trek* was not a significant part of the phenomenon (Jenkins 1992; Bacon-Smith 1992). That is to say, cult activity surrounding *Star Trek* operated as a bottom-up event; subcultural activities created the demand for the *Star Trek* films and other commercial tie-ins. For *thirtysomething*, the reverse (top-down) tendency has operated: the program was conceptualized as an overall marketing phenomenon; attempts to stir up nostalgia for the show came from the corporation that owned the trademark licensing privileges.[6]

According to Lenny Heller, the idea for merchandising around *thirtysomething* was suggested to him by a salesman in the garment center (Seventh Avenue) where Lenny had long been known as a connection maker, someone who had "world production knowledge" and was expert at finding factories for importers. Although Lenny Heller had seen the show and admired its look, he was not a "religious viewer." But when his "finder" put the question to him, "How does the name 'thirtysomething' hit you?" according to Lenny, "I did not sleep that weekend."[7] What struck Lenny was not so much the show itself as the word "thirtysomething," and he is very clear that what he purchased from MGM was the concept of "thirtysomething" rather than the show itself. To put it in the combined languages of copyright law and cultural studies, Lenny Heller purchased the intellectual property "thirtysomething" as a floating signifier that could leave the body of the show it named and attach itself freely to commodities. But he did not purchase a commodity; he purchased the concept. Like the term "yuppie," to which it bears a close family resemblance, "thirtysomething" was not exactly a demographic group or a generational term but rather conveyed an attitude, a spirit, and a way of dressing that symbolizes that attitude. Advertising directors (for Nissan and other products advertised on the show) loved the show and considered it "the best thing they had going" because they were able to target their audience precisely: young, upscale families and singles who were educated and aware—that is to say, yuppies. According to Lenny, all those involved in the commercial end of the show used the yup word "freely and without embarrassment." Thus Lenny, who describes himself as "a very young grandfather," nevertheless feels that his fashion style is very "thirtysomething." The "finder" who suggested the idea to Lenny conceptualized "thirtysomething" as "a name on a label."

When Lenny Heller picked up the license from MGM, he immediately began to sever the signification of the name from the signification of the program, as he puts it, a "distancing of the consumer." Eventually *thirtysomething* would leave its televisual body and come to rest in the pages of a direct-mail catalog. This was a good thing, because Lenny's original marketing plan depended on the show's still being on the air. His original concept was to manufacture a line of clothing with the show's fashion designer, Patrick Norris, retained as the line's "design overseer" while still designing for the show. Lenny planned a fashion show (an "upbeat, upscale fashion presentation") for the New York Hilton that would convey the "flavor" Norris's designs gave the show and went to Asia to manufacture the clothes (followed closely by camera crews from CNN and *Nova*). He took orders from Macy's and Saks for thirtysomething "shops within a shop" in both men's and women's apparel departments in the retail stores, a concept similar to Ralph Lauren and Perry Ellis boutiques.

Lenny admits to having been "shocked" when ABC canceled *thirtysomething*. In response, he attempted to create a market for his catalog by creating a "grass-roots" organization called the Fash'n Fun

thirtysomething™

thirtysomething catgalog sponsors
fash'n fun club inc.

"Bring back **thirtysomething**"
"Bring back **thirtysomething**"

That is the cry that we have been hearing for the past year and a half, and we, the "thirtysomething" apparel catalog, have been listening.

It's time to act. No more crying. No more listening. Together, all of us together, let's do it.

Let us bring back "thirtysomething."

One way or another...In some form or other...It will be done. But we cannot do it alone. Singularly our voice is not strong enough. Clout is based on the law of large numbers.

Now there is **fash'n fun** club inc. and through this national membership club, we will be heard. One of the goals of the **fash'n fun** club is to build so substantial and so powerful a base and warchest, that its demands to bring back **thirtysomething** must be met. The writers, the producers, the network, and all, will take notice.

We, the **thirtysomething** apparel catalog, are proud of this association with the **fash'n fun** club and are delighted to be a charter sponsor. The club has an amazing program - one that all America will appreciate and enjoy. You will learn more by reading the enclosed literature. We love it. We endorse it. And we encourage you to join the club now.

Aside from the fact that your voice is so important in the club's effort to bring back **thirtysomething**, you will also enjoy the many benefits of membership in the club. Obviously your enrollment is also important to us. So in addition to the good stuff offered by the club, we will present the following free gifts as incentives for your joining the **fash'n fun** club now.

1. **thirtysomething** tape cassette soundtrack.
   From the opening theme of the show and throughout the memorable events of the characters' lives, composers Snuffy Walden and Stewart Levin bring the personal experiences of thirtysomething to this cassette. You will hear much of the music on the T.V. show including a new single version of the theme song and songs by Ray Charles and Rickie Lee Jones.

2. **thirtysomething** Stories.
   A 431 page Pocket Books publication which features nine scripts from the show, introduced by their creators - an unforgettable look at Michael, Hope, Elliot, Nancy, Gary, Ellyn, Melissa, and Miles. We savor on the page the experiences that mirror our lives. Just as the show moves us, angers us, makes us laugh, thirtysomething Stories provides the perfect way to relive these moments.

3. **thirtysomething** baseball cap.
   Adjustable cotton twill cap for his/her fit with the "thirtysomething" logo. What a nice and fun way to announce that you are an expression lifestyle and attitude... and a member of the club.

4. **thirtysomething** catalog gift certificate.
   This certificate is good for 20% off on any two items you will order from the very next **thirtysomething** catalog that you will receive.

Obviously the total value of these incentive giveaways will amount to far more than the enrollment fee to join the **fash'n fun** club inc.

We look forward to welcoming you to this club which we so wholeheartedly support. Thank you.

2875 So. Congress Avenue • Suite E • Delray Beach, FL 33445 • (407) 243-3030 • fax (407) 276-7277 • 1-800-528-3320

Club, whose flyer was sent out to all those who had inquired about the catalog. The purpose of the club was to buy products related to the show and, for Apparel Resources, to create a ground-swell demand to bring back the show. However, when MGM objected to the club, Lenny Heller abandoned it in favor of selling his wares direct to the consumer via print and (in the future) home video catalogs. He wants to move "away from the show and toward fashion" while still believing in the power of the show's name. Eventually there would be three *thirtysomething* catalogs, the original pen and ink one followed by two full-color visually pleasing *Sharper Image*–like versions in 1992 and 1993. Textual analysis of the catalog and club mailings reveals interesting connections both to the show and to the idea of yuppie culture discussed in previous chapters. The "Gary jacket," for instance, offered in the catalog, drives home my point that the choice between Michael and Gary is not just one of values but of fashion statements.

What does all of this have to do with modern art? It seems to me that it epitomizes what happened in the eighties when artists who considered themselves modernists and who believed in the purity of art had to make their art under conditions not of their own choosing. While the "creatives" might wish to offer a critique of yuppiedom via their narrative art, such a critique would of necessity come into conflict with

99   Art Discourse in 1980s Television

the needs of capital necessary to produce the show. One doesn't, that is, produce a weekly TV series in a garret or even on an art-house cinema budget. Eventually, the modernist conflict between the artist's desire to create a new language outside of capitalism and the reliance on capitalism for the very production of the work would be thematized in *thirtysomething* and in fact come to occupy the center of its "vision," its portrait of the artist as a young yuppie. In this sense, the demands of the eighties greatly intensified the dilemma of early-twentieth-century modernist artists who could paint in poverty or put on ballets at the Central High School of Needle Trades (the venue for the 1946 premiere of Balanchine's modernist ballet *The Four Temperaments*, choreographed to a commissioned modernist score by Paul Hindemith; see *Choreography by George Balanchine* 1984, p. 175).

The significant art forms of the Reagan era demanded huge infusions of capital: for restaurants, for design, for film production. They could never be pure. And yet "yuppie art" is not a contradiction in terms, if we consider that the production of modernist art in the eighties must inevitably confront a postmodern mode of production. As Frith and Horne put it in their study of art school students in Britain who become pop musicians, "What this suggests to us is not that we are all now colonized by advertisers' fantasies, but that the interplay of artifice and authenticity is central to everyone's lives in consumer capitalism" (1987, p. 180). This awareness of their own postmodern sensibility characterizes three other aesthetically significant television programs of the eighties as well: *Miami Vice* (1984–1989), *Moonlighting* (1985–1989), and *Max Headroom* (1987).

Indeed there already exists a substantial body of academic criticism on the first two of these, and the third would also inspire voluminous commentary were its texts more readily available. Of the three, *Moonlighting* appears most easily assimilated to a concept of postmodernism as complicitous critique. *Miami Vice*—although defined as postmodern in other ways—may at first appear to lack a critical edge. But ultimately I shall argue for the significance of *Max Headroom* as the prototype of postmodern TV.

Moonlighting

In his article on *Moonlighting*, Philip Hayward argues that far from being critical or deconstructive in the old sense, *Moonlighting* was designed to keep engaged the quickened media sensibilities of the baby boom (yuppie) generation:

Instead of dreams of radical, analytically deconstructive television the media mutation of the late Eighties has followed hot on the prophecy of theory and witnessed an eclectic pillaging of once esoteric formal devices, pressing them into forms of popular cultural bricolage glacially unconcerned with niceties of radical schools or purist debates. *Moonlighting*'s strength, originality and challenge to aspects of avant garde (and/or alternative) media practice is in its subtle inter-textualities and formal devices being produced for a popular TV audience, within its own paradigms and with none of the cares of the avant garde and no allegiance to any movement or practice beyond that of populism. (Hayward 1990, p. 266)

This analysis strikes me as curious on a number of levels. As an analysis of the relationship between video practice and politics, it appears to be saying that only the avant-garde can be politically correct. That is to say, as soon as a practice or set of techniques becomes popular, the same techniques automatically become reactionary. As I have been arguing, yuppie television of the eighties tries to interpellate an *elite* subject; it is difficult to see how a show like *Moonlighting* could be described as "populist" at all, at least in comparison to the entire spectrum of programming on U.S. network television at the time. There is a knee-jerk association between populism and right-wing ideology. But it is hard to imagine how one could interpret *Moonlighting* as right wing or even without "cares," given its well-publicized and self-consciously troubled production history. Indeed one could alternatively argue that in foregrounding its own production difficulties, the show thematized the very dilemma that Hayward critiques: what happens when avant-garde practices enter into the very heart of the language of a popular television program? Perhaps in its continual autodeconstruction, *Moonlighting* did more than any other program of the eighties (and for a larger audience) to penetrate the contradictions involved in the commodification of U.S. television as a whole. As Hayward well analyzes, in its ultimate self-reflexive episode, "The Straight Poop," *Moonlighting* foregrounds its own construction. In this pastiched episode, real-life celebrity reporter Rona Barrett inquires into the (quasi-fictionalized) production delays on the show itself. As Hayward writes,

The Straight Poop's scenario was inspired by Press publicity about the alleged (real-life) friction between Shepherd and Willis during production of the series. The episode therefore constitutes an attempt to represent this within the series; but significantly, in attempting to refer out to this off-screen publicity, had to abandon the traditional representational role and further complicate matters by a logical slippage where the David/Maddie characters were represented as responsible for the dispute which prevented filming of the show (which is of course an extra-textual function fulfilled by the "real-life" Shepherd and Willis characters). Thus David and Maddie effectively acted Willis and Shepherd acting David and Maddie as themselves (!)—this being further compounded by the appearance of the *real-life* former husband of Shepherd (director Peter Bogdanovich) appearing in the narrative as a former lover of the fictional Maddie character but also referring to another ex-romance of his with a *model from Memphis*— Shepherd in her *real-life* role. This *slippage* within the episode affects a clearly identifiable transgression of both conventional representation (the separation of signifier and signified) and a collapse in the surface-depth model; which both testifies to the acuity of Jameson's analysis of the advanced commodification of cultural artifacts and demonstrates how audiences' perceptions and understandings have undergone a quiet and complementary shift symmetrical with that of cultural production. (Hayward 1990, p. 273; italics in original)

This lengthy quotation both describes the episode and reveals how difficult such an episode is to describe in words. And yet the experience of the episode is pleasurable; it is not in the least inaccessible. The end credits even interweave "bloopers" for our enjoyment, as we see David and Maddie (or is it Shepherd and Willis?) shopping for the "*Miami Vice* look."

Miami Vice (1984-1989)

Among intellectuals still committed to liberal humanist and even modernist/Marxist conceptions of critique, *Miami Vice* proved a troubling postmodern text. Michael Pollan contrasts *Miami Vice*'s visual innovations with the "literary sophistication" and "realism" pioneered by *Hill Street Blues* earlier in the decade, referring to this development as "sensation television" (Pollan 1985, p. 54). By this he means a new kind of visual orientation not bound by "old-fashioned literary concerns [such as] logic, plausibility, the whole bland business of cause and effect." Todd Gitlin, following Jameson, refers to the show's "studied blankness of tone," its emphasis on "surface" (Gitlin 1987, p. 143). Both critics cite with amazement and dismay producer Michael Mann's oracular reply when asked what was distinctive about the show: "No earth tones." In short, humanist critics of varying persuasions have seen in *Miami Vice* the end of criticism as they have known it in a total, numbing, thought-dulling complicity emblematic of the Reagan era. Yet the very qualities that go against critique at the level of narrative placed *Miami Vice* at the center of postmodern art. *Miami Vice* in fact was often unreadable at the level of narrative or, worse, readable as a mainstream, sexist cop show whose premise was unbelievable and whose terrible plotting somehow never managed to emerge as an emblem of art discourse as it had for *thirtysomething*. In addition, *Miami Vice* featured more overtly political content than did most other contemporary television pro-grams—certainly *Moonlighting* never dealt with U.S. involvement in Nicaragua as does the "Stone's War" episode of *Miami Vice*. Somehow the show's narrative incoherence and postmodern style prevented most critics from reading it as complicitous critique.

But does not the show's very reliance on visual excess and sexual dis-play lead to a kind of critique? Let's look, for example, at a classically Hollywood classically scopophilic opening that pastiches—or does it parody?—the spider woman figure from film noir. The postcredits se-quence of "Definitely Miami" finds Crockett and Tubbs poolside at a Miami deco hotel on a sweltering day. In a sequence through-com-posed to a languid tropical horn solo, guest star Arielle Dombasle (known to the art house audience for her role as the bikini-clad "older woman" in Eric Rohmer's *Pauline at the Beach*) visually seduces Crockett, Tubbs, and the (implied) male spectator of the sequence. A series of glance/object shots between the men and the French seduc-tress would seem to position this scene squarely in the center of the Hollywood visual discourse of the male gaze. At first glance this would appear to be yet another classic instance of the fetishization of the fe-male body by the male gaze, and indeed it is easily interpreted as such out of context by male undergraduates. This possibility of complicity is always a part of postmodern art. But it is too much, and too self-aware. The male gaze is drawn out and exaggerated by slow motion, a panning shot over the woman's body and a series of dissolves. The vice cops' conversation during this "stakeout" also reveals a knowingness about modern art unlikely to be possessed by the young men who would leer and hoot at this sequence. When Crockett says, "I hate the waiting; I feel like a character in a Beckett play," Tubbs replies, "Since when do you know Beckett?" And Sonny's knowing rejoinder is "Charlie Beckett,

down on the corner, the shoeshine, writes plays on the side." During the "male gaze" sequence, the men make jokes about eyestrain.

A postmodern reading reveals the sequence to be entirely complicit with sexism and yet entirely schooled in feminist film theory. The body of the woman is treated visually as a commercial; the urbanity of the men is acknowledged in the modernist allusion to Beckett, only to be undercut by the postmodern joke on the modernist allusion. The woman too knows her Freud and clearly controls the situation, as her return of the glance reveals. In case we missed the point, a young male body is present for the homoerotic or feminine gaze of the spectator. In every carefully wrought frame, the sequence is both totally complicitous and totally self-critical. As with earlier literary and filmic forms of modernist allusion, what is radical is the show's relationship to prior examples of its own genre and medium. Whether or not the viewer gets the joke depends on circumstances outside of the text.

Max Headroom (U.S., 1987)

In spite of its seemingly poor showing on U.S. network television, *Max Headroom* had an impact far in excess of its ratings as a "cult" show (and it should be remembered that even a ratings failure such as this had an average viewership of six million weekly households).[8] Its genre—dystopic science fiction—although a popular one in 1980s cinema (*Blade Runner*, 1982; *Brazil*, 1985; *Robocop*, 1987), was hardly a genre suited to the needs of prime-time television, whose vision of the future—à la *Star Trek*—tended to be a utopian one. *Max Headroom* appears even more critical when you take into consideration its image of a world "twenty minutes into the future" as one controlled by giant television networks whose concept of citizenship-as-ratings even the FCC might deplore. Arguably *Max Headroom* is the televisual equivalent to Baudrillard's theory of the simulacrum and the silent masses—in one program from the second season, the entire world becomes addicted to a ridiculous game show called "Wackets" that has been programmed to trigger endorphins in the unsuspecting viewer, stimulating deep pleasure and the desire for repeated consumption. In Baudrillard's words: "They retain a fascination for the medium which they prefer to the critical exigencies of the message. For fascination is not dependent on meaning, it is proportional to the disaffection of meaning" (1983, p. 35). Because it is able to actually depict the universe of the simulacrum, *Max Headroom* may in the long run prove a more valuable form of social critique than Baudrillard's outmoded, still-too-rationalistic print texts. Achieving popularity in the United States at about the same time, Max Headroom, the first computer-generated TV star, and Jean Baudrillard, author of what's been called "the first radical high-tech, new wave social theory" (Kellner 1989, p. 84), may actually prove to be—in true sci fi fashion—identical twins separated at birth.

Both *Max Headroom* and the episode of *Moonlighting* cited above make use of the modernist practice of calling attention to the materiality of the text by exposing its means of signification—a typically Brechtian critical technique. I would like to explore what this means by considering the use of "noise" in the programs. The "noise dissolve" between shots and as a transition between program and ad segments, and the revelation of the leader with its offscreen extradiegetic voice are age-old staples of experimental film. As with the use of such techniques in avant-garde practice, the noise dissolve does foreground the materiality of the text. But is this necessarily or was it ever critical? Does it not also celebrate the wonders of technology? In the world twenty minutes into the future, forgotten men stare at fuzz on their ubiquitous TV monitors, just as we often do today. The noise dissolve is both deconstructive and complicitous, both critical of television's realist conventions and complicitous in becoming itself conventional in subsequent episodes of the series.

The U.S. *Max Headroom* is based on a British version; arguably the critique and view of the future presented is far more applicable to the

United States, which already possesses a conception of democracy as the achievement of high ratings. In fact, as I will argue, the British version presents what I will call a "modernist" critique from a position outside the program; the U.S. series—taken in its entire flow—presents a "postmodernist" critique—one whose complicity places it inside the text.

In the brilliant pilot episode based on the British version, the program *Max Headroom* critiques Network 23 for endangering lives through "blipverting" TV's version of Baudrillard's masses. The next week and in subsequent episodes, the very blipvert for the Zigzag Corporation that was the subject of TV journalist Edison Carter's triumphant crusade and the impetus for Max's creation will be incorporated into the front credits for the program—now addressed to us as spectators/consumers. But the pilot episode blipverts us in yet another way. Its credits go so far as to reveal the place marker for the commercial—"place network commercial here"—except that it is Network 23's commercial, not *Max Headroom*'s. In the diegesis, the purpose of the blipverts was to keep the audience from changing stations during ads by barraging them with information. The humanistic discourse of the program—with Edison's evocation of the traditional TV hero triumphing in his quest for truth, justice, and the American way—represents the end of the plot but not the end of the text.

For the flow pattern at the end of *Max Headroom* does not allow the spectator to distinguish easily among program segments and advertising segments; it is not always clear from which diegetic space Max has emerged—the narrative of the program, the space of a commentary on that narrative, the space of previews of future narratives, or the space of the commercial. The constant appearance of Max blurs the boundaries between the program and the Coke ad in which Max exhorts the masses not to say the "P" word. Moreover, the character of Max appeared in Coke ads prior to having his own ABC show. Conceived for a British TV movie, the computer-generated Max was spread to the United States on an interview show on the cable channel Cinemax and from there to heavy use in Coke ads. As was true of commercials spun off from *Dynasty*, the Max Coke ads often appeared in the space between the end of *Max Headroom* and the end credits. In one such instance, Edison Carter, the TV journalist of the future, pokes his microphone at the villain, demanding the truth about blipverts; in the ad that follows the show, an American father pokes his microphone at his children, demanding the truth about Pizza Hut. This parallel ad is followed by the well-known "Cokeolo-

gists" convention spot that introduced Max to America. Andrew Ross
has described the ad:

> Take for example the TV ads for New Coke (dir. Ridley Scott)
> which featured Max on a vast video screen as the star attraction
> at a "cokeologists' convention" attended by thousands of cheering,
> video-happy teenagers. These ads were a direct riposte to the
> highly successful "Pepsi generation" ads featuring "live" appear-
> ances by such megastars as Michael Jackson, David Bowie, Lionel
> Richie, Tina Turner and Don Johnson. Despite their "leading-
> edge" meanings, the Pepsi ads adopted the traditional manner of
> establishing a demographic community of consumers bound to-
> gether by association with celebrities whom they themselves have
> helped to make famous. The Max Headroom ads, which fronted
> Coca-Cola's attempts to promote New Coke, could be read as an
> inside joke shared by the audience about the fake or artificial con-
> struction of celebrity, as well as the audience's collusive role in that
> process. (Ross 1990, p. 149)

It is important to note that Max Headroom's incarnation as
spokesperson for Coca-Cola preceded his appearance as the star of a
weekly series; in this instance the adage that, for U.S. television, the
programming is an ad for the commercials bears a quite literal
meaning. Indeed, since the Max Headroom premiere on ABC also featured the Pepsi ad in which a fast food restaurant comes to a halt when

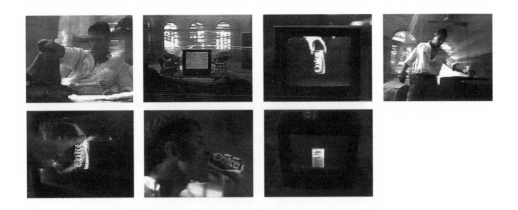

a young man tries to order Coke instead of Pepsi, one might posit that the cola wars are the programming for which *Max Headroom* is the commercial. Even from an auteurist standpoint, the ads are more significant than the program: while the program quotes from dystopic sci fi films such as *Blade Runner* and *Brazil*, the Coke ads are actually directed by *Blade Runner*'s director, Ridley Scott. Michael and Elliot could not have asked for more.

The second *Max Headroom*/Coca-Cola spot I will describe is perhaps the most amazing ad ever to appear on American television and a high point of postmodern art of the eighties. Appearing during an internal break in the second episode, the commercial does not feature Max Headroom but rather the new computer-savvy consumer-spectator/subject of the eighties, perhaps the "new man" that Gitlin described as the addressee of car commercials during the Reagan era. In the thirty-second commercial, which has only one line of "dialogue," an announcer's voice-over, a male yuppie languishes on a hot day in front of his TV set, in a loft apartment cooled only by a fan attached to the cathedral ceiling and an obviously not very satisfying can of Pepsi. After zapping a few politicians, the sweating yuppie puts down his can of Pepsi, becoming transfixed by the can of New Coke appearing on his screen. In an astonishing moment of commodity self-consciousness, the yuppie reaches into the TV set and extracts the Coke. The announcer's voice tells us, "When you're searching for something better, more modern, refreshing, tune in to the taste of New Coke." As the yuppie zaps off the Pepsi can with his remote control, the announcer tells us to "catch the wave—Coke." It is not possible to say which has priority: the introduction of Max Headroom as a new type of computer-generated television star or the introduction of New Coke as a new kind of soft drink for future generations. Neither had any lasting success, although one imagines that Max Headroom will be remembered by critics long after the too sweet taste of the ill-timed New Coke has been displaced forever by the nostalgic perfection of Classic Coca-Cola. Or could we say that the cola wars were the most significant historical event of the decade in terms of postmodern art?

The British *Max Headroom* functions as an excellent "control." Having used a very similar script and a lower-tech but similar mise-en-scène and even though it preceded the American version, it nevertheless cannot be postmodern in the manner of the American version, for it does not foreground its own complicity—it can't without being broadcast on the American system with its interdiegetic flow between programs and ads. In many respects the British version is more of a critique in the modernist/Marxist sense of the term. But in other ways, it is not. For instance, the American version quotes a line from the British one: "How can you tell when a politician is lying? He moves his lips." But for the U.S. version, it is Max himself who appears on monitors throughout the dystopian city, and his line is changed from "politicians" to "our network president." The critique is less of society in general than of the television institution. And yet, which version is the more radically artistic—the *Max Headroom* that is about its own complicity in a future demonstrably already here (we have seen the Coke ads) or an incisive yet distant critical glance at somebody else's future?

All of these shows are about their own positioning in television's flow; without being situated as such they would lose their critical edge along with their complicity with the material needs of capitalism. The Coke ads on *Max Headroom* are not only part of the flow; they are part of the text conceptualized as postmodern rather than modernist. It is this postmodern textuality that unites such diverse shows as *thirtysomething, Moonlighting, Miami Vice,* and *Max Headroom* into a common "moment," during which they came to represent the artistic peak of American television network programming in its last moments of unity at the end of the Reagan era. It could thus be said that postmodern TV of the eighties constituted an art movement but one so different from the usual "avant-garde" art movements of the twentieth century that we failed to recognize it as such.

Notes

1 Note the publication dates on the following books about Woody Allen, film artist: Robert Benayoun (1986), *The Films of Woody Allen* (Harmony Books); Douglas

Brode (1991), *The Films of Woody Allen* (Carol Publishing Group); Sam B. Girgus (1993), *The Films of Woody Allen* (Cambridge University Press); Lee Guthrie (1978), *Woody Allen: A Biography* (Drake Publishers); Foster Hirsch (1981), *Love, Sex, Death and the Meaning of Life: Woody Allen's Comedy* (McGraw-Hill); Diane Jacobs (1982), *But We Need the Eggs: The Magic of Woody Allen* (St. Martin's Press); Eric Lax (1991), *Woody Allen: A Biography* (Knopf); Graham McCann (1990), *Woody Allen: New Yorker* (Polity); Thierry de Navacelle (1987), *Woody Allen on Location* (Morrow); Nancy Pogel (1987), *Woody Allen* (Twayne); Stephen J. Spignesi (1992), *The Woody Allen Companion* (Andrews and McMeel); Annette Wernblad (1992), *Brooklyn Is Not Expanding: Woody Allen's Comic Universe* (Fairleigh Dickinson University Press); Maurice Yacowar (1991), *Loser Take All : The Comic Art of Woody Allen* (new expanded edition; originally published in 1979) (Ungar).

2 Discussed at length alongside Fellini's *8 ½* by Robert Stam (1992, pp. 155–159).

3 We find it in *The Wizard of Oz*, for example.

4 Not only was this classic film remade for TV starring Marlo Thomas, it was also remade to fit the needs of various series and serials, most notably a special episode of the soap opera *Santa Barbara*.

5 This analysis is based on the broadcast version, which differs in some ways from the published script (primarily in that some scenes in the script did not appear in the broadcast).

6 Later, I will complicate this bottom-up/top-down distinction, but for now it seems useful.

7 This and subsequent information and quotations are from a most enjoyable telephone conversation with Leonard Heller on 1 June 1994 (Heller 1994).

8 Based on numbers provided by Nielsen Media Research to the author.

5

Serial Form, Melodrama,
and Reaganite Ideology
in Eighties TV

When quality TV looks to its roots in serial form, it tends to invoke the serial tradition of the British "classic serial" imports popular on PBS, such as *Upstairs, Downstairs; Brideshead Revisited;* and *The Jewel in the Crown*. However, there is another, native serial tradition to which the prime-time quality serial of the 1980s is even more indebted: the tradition of daytime continuing drama or soap opera. Not surprisingly, this is a debt that the creators of these shows would rather erase. This chapter will explain why the prime-time quality serial wants to deny this link to the most popular form of drama of the 1980s: the continuing melodramatic serial. Although one claims to be art, the other trash, they share in common a tendency that pervaded American television of the 1980s: serialization.

If one takes a sweeping view of narrative modes, it is easy to see how diverse critics ranging from literary to postmodern to *TV Guide* have classified all of American television drama as "melodrama." If, as David Thorburn has written, all television acting is "operatic" (1994, pp. 537–550), then soap opera acting must be positively Wagnerian. *American Film* quotes Marshall Herskovitz: "Let's face it, a lot of the conventions in episodic television are moribund. The heightened, operatic method of storytelling has become old" (Lantos 1987, p. 51). Sasha Torres deals with the extent to which the show and its creators want to identify with a tradition of realism all the while fulfilling many definitions of melodrama, especially the idea of a bourgeois subject matter addressed from one bourgeois to another (1989, p. 88).

Along the same lines, although for a very different audience, an insightful and rather scholarly article in *Soap Opera Digest* titled "Is Your Favorite Primetime Show a Soap?" (Hoke-Kahwaty 1990, pp. 24–29) concludes that in many respects *thirtysomething* resembles daytime soap opera more than do other prime-time continuing dramas such as *L.A. Law* or *Wiseguy*. Following TV critic Horace Newcomb, the article differentiates among episodic shows, cumulative narratives, "arc" shows, mutiple-story shows, and soap operas, making the point that most prime-time shows after the 1960s employed some elements of continuing drama, if only in the sense that Jean Stapleton's character on *All in the Family* grew from a fifties woman to a seventies woman. According to Newcomb, as quoted in the article, a better name for the series-with-a-memory concept would be a "cumulative narrative" (p. 27). Although shows of this narrative type such as *China Beach* possess a sense of history, they still wrap up stories in one episode. By contrast, the "arc" show, epitomized by Stephen Cannell's *Wiseguy*, uses short-term (two- to ten-episode) story lines in addition to continuing story lines involving the main characters. The multiple story line shows pioneered by Stephen Bochco (such as *Hill Street Blues* and *L.A. Law*) combine arc and soap: all stories are not resolved at once. According to Newcomb "*thirtysomething* is the most soapy of all the arc shows. It doesn't want to be called a soap because of the [perceived] inferior social status" (p. 27).

Newcomb's comment stands in stark contrast to the protests of the cast of *thirtysomething* about calling their show a soap. The bone of contention tends to be that soap operas are all plot, whereas quality serials focus on "relationships." Putting aside for a moment the truth value of this claim,[1] it might more accurately be said that *thirtysomething* claims art status and takes pride in being badly plotted relative to the more Aristotelian structure of daytime soap opera. For example, after twenty-one episodes, Hope and Michael finally resolve the dilemma of the pilot by going away for a weekend! In the December 1988 season opener, Michael and Elliot's secretary quits, thus resolving the dilemma of the first season's third episode over whether or not to dismiss her. Some episodes follow story arcs; others are episodic or episodic with minor continuities of story arcs; for example, whether to invite Elliot or Nancy to Janie's birthday. The fact that *thirtysomething* is so badly plotted clues the yuppie spectator to separate the show from soap opera and to make of its random seriality an art discourse.

thirtysomething also used a type of scene construction common to daytime soaps. For example, in alternating scenes, Hope/Nancy and Elliot/Michael discuss Nancy and Elliot's having had sex—they echo each other's words. This kind of parallelism is both arty and soapy at the same time. By the time the camping trip promised in the first episode occurs, the m/f parallelism of narrative has become so established that it is inevitable that the women would go and the men stay home (to work). These frequent splits between men discussing power and women relationships follow the pattern of *Dallas* and daytime. In

fact, *Dynasty* crossed spheres more than *thirtysomething* did in terms of showing women actually *acting* in the public sphere. In an article about Joan Collins and active female spectatorship, Belinda Budge does a feminist reading of Alexis as a positive role model because she highlights contradictions within melodrama and patriarchy (1989, pp. 102–11). Thus she represents a pleasurable image of a newer, "wilder" woman not completely bound by the male gaze. The analysis emphasizes the activity of female audiences.

Yet by dealing with yuppie representations addressed to a yuppie spectator within an art discourse, *thirtysomething*'s image belied the fact that it addressed the same concerns for its core audience that daytime does for a broader female population. For the yuppie audience, *thirtysomething* was precisely a soap opera, if only because of its emphasis on the personal sphere and the rhythms of everyday life for an ensemble cast. Although *thirtysomething* used soap opera form in order to chronicle the dissolution of the family in one sense, it also used the mini-resolutions of the form to frame tableaux of a new kind of family portrait more suited to the *Big Chill* generation.

Above all what relates *thirtysomething* to soap opera is its reliance on a core family involved in ongoing conflicts at home and at work: that is to say, serial narrative and melodramatic subject matter.

Quality TV of the eighties thus qualifies as melodrama without being melodramatic in the pejorative sense of the term. Sasha Torres comments, "[Producer Edward] Zwick's efforts to oppose *thirtysomething* to melodrama by aligning the show with realism are undermined not only by the series' intermittent anti-realism, but also by the fact that both realism and melodrama may be employed to depict domestic detail" (Torres 1989, p. 89). As prime-time serial dramas, quality shows such as *thirtysomething* and *L.A. Law* link up directly with the tendency toward serialization that dominated television drama of the Reagan era, whether it took the form of so-called realism or of melodrama.

What Peter Brooks calls the everyday connotations of the term melodrama—"the indulgence of strong emotionalism; moral polarization and schematization; extreme states of being, situations, action; overt villainy, persecution of the good, and final reward of virtue; inflated and extravagant expression; dark plottings, suspense, breathtaking peripety" (1976, pp. 11–12)—uncannily predicts a form of programming practically unique to American television of the Reagan years: the prime-time continuing melodramatic serial.

Prior to the 1980s, serial melodrama was overwhelmingly a daytime form; the only successful prime-time example was *Peyton Place* (1964–1969), the film versions of which (*Peyton Place* and *Return to Peyton Place*) belonged to the 1950s melodrama.[2] Prime-time television of the 1970s offered no equivalent to the film melodramas of the 1950s to mid-1960s recently rescued from obscurity by film theorists. During the Reagan era, however, domestic melodrama encroached upon the domain of the sitcom and the cop show. It would not be controversial to note that domestic melodrama has thrived as a popular media form for adult women precisely during the two political periods in postwar America characterized as ideologically stable and virulently pro-family: the Eisenhower and Reagan presidencies. The sheer proliferation of prime-time serial melodramas on 1980s network TV is impressive, especially if you include the short-lived attempts at the form with the decade-long popular shows such as *Dallas* (CBS, 1978–1991), *Falcon Crest* (CBS, 1981–1990), *Dynasty* (ABC, 1981–1989), and *Knot's Landing* (CBS, 1979–1993).[3] By 1990, only three prime-time soap operas remained: *Dallas, Knot's Landing*, and *Twin Peaks. Dallas* had fallen drastically in the ratings and would soon conclude, while its spin-off *Knot's Landing*, still popular, was noted for its middle-class orientation; this show began to sink in 1991–1992 and concluded its long run in 1993. The short-lived *Twin Peaks*, with its auteurist director and postmodernist bent, signaled a very different kind of cult serial than its 1980s cousins. In the nineties, prime-time serial drama is emerging as a teen and young adult form with the Fox Network programs *Beverly Hills 90210*, *Melrose Place*, and their clones, but these are not mass audience (and international) top-ten hits, nor are they as pervasive as serials were during the eighties.[4] During the period in which the prime-time serial emerged, daytime soap operas skyrocketed, having risen to an astonishing peak of popularity at the time of Luke and Laura's wedding in 1981, yet ten years later the networks were worried about the decline in overall viewing figures for daytime drama (*Soap Opera Digest* 1991, p. 33). By the nineties, serial melodrama had reached the parodic extremes of the Energizer pink bunny ads, and the mise-en-scène of prime-time soap operas had been remaindered into serialized Tasters' Choice coffee commercials.

Such are the "facts" on the rise and fall of serial melodrama on American television. What it all means, however, is debatable and will form the subject of this chapter. The dominance of domestic melodramatic serials was not purely quantitative, it was also aesthetic and ideological. That is to say, serial form was the aesthetically dominant narrative innovation of the decade, while the typical conflicts of domestic melodrama came to represent the decade's central ideology in the way it condenses the corporation and the family—the mainstay institutions of Reaganism—into a single representational unit in the form of what I will call the "corporate family." But should we assume that domestic melodrama *as a form* is itself inherently conservative?

Theories of Film Melodrama

In literature and film studies, melodrama has repeatedly been theorized as creating an *excess*, whether defined as a split between the level of narrative and that of mise-en-scène or as a form of "hysteria," the visually articulated return of the ideologically repressed. Despite changing theoretical stances, critics have viewed this excess not merely as aesthetic but as ideological, opening up a textual space which may be read against the seemingly hegemonic surface.[5]

The key text for the theorization of visual excess has tended to be Douglas Sirk's *Written on the Wind,* with its intricately layered (and thus visually ruptured) mirror shots, phallic symbolism and "hysterical" montage. Oil-dynasty sagas from the 1950s melodramatic tradition— *Giant* and *Written on the Wind* (both 1956 releases)—provided prototypes for *Dallas* and *Dynasty.* The iconography of the oil baron's mansion with its massive central staircase comes directly from these films. In each of the two melodramatic traditions, the disintegration of a capitalist ruling class family is figured by hysterical confrontations within the family manse, often taking place on the very staircase that signifies the grandeur and unity of the dynastic family. In *Written on the Wind* (top illustration), in the oft-noted hysterical montage sequence, the wayward daughter dances seductively in her boudoir as the paterfamilias succumbs to a heart attack while climbing the massive staircase. Thirty years later, Blake Carrington attempts to strangle Alexis on a similar staircase in the disputed Carrington mansion as part of the 1986 season cliffhanger for *Dynasty*. Each scene is fully within the melodramatic tradition of excess, accompanied by blaring music and operatic acting. Unlike Sirk's other melodramas and also unlike daytime soap operas prior to the eighties, *Written on the Wind, Dallas,* and *Dynasty* focus on the capitalist ruling elite rather than the bourgeois family. The address is not so uniformly from one bourgeois to another as it is in other forms of melodrama (as noted by Nowell-Smith 1977, p. 117), although of course the representation of the upper classes is intended to be read by a bourgeois audience. More than any other Sirk film, *Written on the Wind* seems to occupy the same excessive representational field as 1980s prime-time serial melodramas.

Reading *Dallas* and *Dynasty*

We need to historicize "excess" that should be viewed relative to the style and medium in which each era of melodrama appears. In this sense, *Dallas* and especially *Dynasty* are in excess of the visual and dramatic norms for prime-time drama of the late 1970s and far in excess of the conventions for mise-en-scène of daytime dramas of the same period. Thus when viewed in terms of their own medium, the seemingly simple mise-en-scène and editing style of the prime-time serials takes on a new signification. Although mise-en-scène in *Dallas* and *Dynasty* does not take on the hysterical dimensions of a Sirk or Fassbinder film, it does seem at the very least opulent compared to other prime-time programs and certainly compared to the daytime soaps. Budgetary considerations alone show the emphasis placed on mise-en-scène. According to one source, "*Dynasty* costs approximately one million dollars an hour because of the show's cavernous and opulent sets, not to mention the dazzling fashions worn by cast members" (*Soap Opera Digest* 1982, p. 141). Although there is nothing inherently subversive about such splendor, it does serve to take the family dynasty serials outside the normal upper-middle-class milieu of most film and television melodrama. The very rich portrayed in these narratives exceed the norms of their audience both economically and morally; luxurious mise-en-scène objectifies such excess. Nevertheless, in order to fulfill the theory that excess leads to a countercurrent in the text, some authorial voice would need to use the visual excess against the narrational level.

In 1983, I argued that this does not happen in TV melodrama, that *Dynasty* had no Douglas Sirk. What I should have said was that (to echo Foucault) the name of the author had not yet been assigned to these texts, either by academic TV analysts or in more popular critical apparati. In this respect, the name of the author confers a special status on texts previously deemed corporate works of mass culture. This is what occurred when, by invoking the name of Douglas Sirk, certain 1950s melodramas were assimilated to the Brechtian tradition. When, in *Sirk on Sirk*, Jon Halliday interviewed the director and discovered that, far from being a Hollywood hack, he was a European intellectual, the status of Sirk's Universal films from the 1950s was greatly enhanced (Sirk 1971). The films were now readable as expressions of the tension between system and author in which Sirk exaggerated the conventions of the Hollywood "weepie" in order to subvert them. Academically, this

The Real Star of 'Dynasty'
Esther Shapiro and Her Empire · By Joe Klein
NEW YORK

naming of an author has never happened for *Dynasty*. Yet in the popular and especially in the yuppie media, cocreator and executive producer Esther Shapiro was nominated for the role. Appearing on the September 2, 1985, cover of *New York* magazine, she sits as a queen amidst the Carrington dynasty. Even the caption points to her mythical status as a media *auteur*, for she appears not with a group of actors but with "Krystle, Blake, and Alexis," the Carringtons themselves. *New York* dubs Esther Shapiro "the real star of Dynasty" (Klein 1985). Moreover, her story follows the exact trajectory of those more literary types referred to as "neoconservative intellectuals" during the Reagan era. In her introduction to the curious volume *Dynasty: The Authorized Biography of the Carringtons*, Shapiro, billed as the "co-creator of the world's most popular television show" on the cover of the *Biography,* claims that all she did was foresee a need for more "romance" in the eighties, admitting that "in the sixties and seventies we had written and produced gritty social dramas—*Sarah T.: Portrait of a Teenage Alcoholic; Intimate Strangers; Minstrel Man; The Cracker Factory*—films that were, we hoped, thematically important and reflective of that period of great turbulence.... 'Important,' 'sensitive,' 'illuminating,' 'real,' 'socially significant,' were words that we searched for in reviews" (1984, p. vi). Her trajectory from the liberal social problem TV movie to the program most symptomatic of the Reagan era prompts me to label Esther Shapiro the great unsung neoconservative intellectual of the 1980s. That she has not achieved this status is more a function of the lowly status of TV entertainment in the culture at large than it is of her role as an intellectual in Gramsci's sense of the term.[6] In charge of miniseries at ABC during the mid-seventies, Shapiro commissioned *Friendly Fire* from Fay Kanin, its writer and coproducer. Later Shapiro would executive produce *Heartbeat* with writer and coproducer Sara Davidson. Her association with other notable "women of the sixties" who would work in television is striking. So is the shift from social-realist liberal 1970s feminism (*Friendly Fire*) to supposed neoconservative kitsch (*Dynasty*) to the curious blend of feminism and sensationalism that characterized *Heartbeat*. Riddled in contradictions, *Heartbeat* was the ultimate yuppie conception of feminism, combining the social consciousness of *Friendly Fire* with the lifestyle emphasis of *Dynasty*.

By reading *Dynasty* as the work of an intentional camp sensibility, seemingly "straight" or purely expressive uses of mise-en-scène might be interpreted in a more Brechtian mode, or at least as evidence of an intentional "intensification" such as Paul Willemen has claimed for Douglas Sirk. Willemen explains Sirk's style as an intensification of generic practices, not as irony per se. Since he had to appeal to a mass audience, Sirk drew on Expressionist and Brechtian theatrical experience "not to break the rules . . . but to intensify them." This was accomplished through the magnification of the emotionality, the use of pathos, choreography, and music, and through aspects of mise-en-scène such as "mirror-ridden walls." Such intensification puts a distance, though not necessarily one perceived by the audience, between "the film and its narrative pretext." Even if not perceived by the mass audience, Willemen argues, distanciation "may still exist within the film itself" (1971, pp. 63–67).

From all the evidence, it is much more likely that contemporary audiences for *Dynasty* perceived its self-mocking tone than that similar audiences did so for Sirk in 1956. Even at the level of mise-en-scène the show's melodramatic excess made such readings probable. For example, an unusually complex "layered" composition in *Dynasty* featured Alexis Carrington in the foreground of the frame arranging flowers in her ex-husband's drawing room as Krystle, her archrival and the current Mrs. Carrington, enters to the rear of the frame carrying an identical flower arrangement. Read "straight," the flowers externalize the emotions of the characters without in any way splitting the perception of the viewer. But from a Brechtian or even a camp perspective,

it is a bit *de trop* to have the current wife and the ex-wife thus compete in floral displays. Another episode of *Dynasty* from the early 1980s featured a classically Oedipal composition as Fallon, the father-fixated daughter, and her father Blake Carrington kiss over her baby's crib as Fallon's husband enters the center of the composition. Later in the decade the infamous "cat fights" between Alexis and Krystle, complete with mud slinging, pond tossing, and clothes ripping, intensify the convention of feminine rivalry so prevalent in the soap opera tradition by turning it into a camp display. Through "hysteria" in the mise-en-scène, "excess" is represented for TV.

Still, it is hard to center excess in prime-time TV on mise-en-scène, for television's limited visual scale places its representational emphasis elsewhere. Acting, editing, musical underscoring, and the use of the zoom lens frequently conspire to create scenes of high (melo)drama, and even more so when these cinematic conventions accompany such Freudian representations as hysteria and the Oedipus complex. Soap opera acting styles also tend toward hysteria.

In fact it is the acting conventions of soap opera, those heightened, operatic methods of storytelling shunned by Herskovitz, that are most often ridiculed for their excess, their seeming to transgress the norms for a "realistic" television acting style. Compared to Peter Brooks's description of melodramatic acting in the nineteenth-century French theater, with its eye rolling and teeth gnashing, acting on TV serials approaches minimalism; nevertheless it appears excessive in comparison to the more naturalistic mode concurrently employed in other forms of television (especially quality TV) and in the cinema, just as the overblown "bad acting" in Sirk's films did for its time (Brooks 1976, p. 47). Yet both forms of melodramatic acting are in keeping with related conventions for distilling and intensifying emotion.

On *Dallas* and *Dynasty*, as on daytime soaps, the majority of scenes consist of intense emotional confrontations between individuals closely related either by blood or by marriage. Most scenes are filmed in medium close-up to give full reign to emotionality without obscuring the decor. The hyperintensity of each confrontation is accentuated by a use of underscoring not found in any other TV genre and by conventions of exchanged glances, shot duration, and the zoom lens. Although television does not often avail itself of the elaborate moving camera and mirror shots Sirk employed in the fifties (and Fassbinder in the seventies) to Brechtian effect, these television techniques appear to serve many of the same functions in terms of exceeding the norms of their medium.

Following and exaggerating a convention of daytime soaps, *Dallas* and *Dynasty* typically hold a shot on the screen for at least a "beat" after the dialogue has ended, usually in combination with shot-reverse shot cuts between the actors' locked gazes. This conventional manner of closing a scene (usually accompanied by a dramatic burst of music) leaves a residue of emotional intensity just prior to a scene change or commercial break. It serves as a form of punctuation, signifying momentary closure, but it also carries meaning within the scene, a meaning connected to the intense interpersonal involvements each scene depicts. Another intensifying technique adapted from daytime drama is the use of zooms-in of varying speeds and durations, with the fast zoom-in to freeze frame being the most dramatic, as when it is used on a close-up of J.R. at the finale of most episodes of *Dallas*. For coding moments of "peak" hysteria, *Dallas* and *Dynasty* employ repeated zooms-in to close-ups of all actors in a scene. Reserved for moments of climactic intensity, this technique was used to create the end of season cliffhanger for the 1981–1982 season of *Dynasty*. In this case the climax was both narrative and sexual, with the zooms used on the injured Blake Carrington intercut with scenes of Alexis Carrington making love to Blake's enemy Cecil Colby. *Dallas* employed a similar device in a scene where J.R. finally accepts his father's death and we zoom repeatedly to a portrait of Jock on the wall at Southfork. *Dynasty* was famous for orchestrating its story lines to a crescendo in the final segments of its year-end cliffhanger. For the 1981–1982 finale, three strands—the kidnaping of Fallon and Jeff's child, Blake's fight with a deranged psychotherapist, and Cecil Colby's heart attack in the midst

of being mounted by Alexis—are woven into a stirring climax. As Alexis slaps the gasping Cecil while shouting, "You can't die. I need you to get Blake," Fallon screams for her daddy, her voice carrying over the image of an unconscious Blake lying prone on a mountaintop as a helpless Krystle attempts to summon him on a walkie-talkie. For the 15 May 1985 Moldavian massacre, an Eisensteinian masterpiece that a colleague of mine uses to teach film editing, time is expanded and motion slowed as the traditional wedding closure becomes the mass slaughter that will emerge as America's hermeneutic question for the summer of 1985 (just as who shot J.R.? had seen us through the summer of 1980). By 1986 the already intensified cliffhangers were starting to camp themselves. As Alexis orders Blake to take his "blond tramp" and leave the Carrington mansion whose deed she now holds, we have evolved into the truly Crawfordesque.

Serial Form and Closure

Despite the similarity of representational field, 1980s prime-time melodrama does not take the same narrative form as *Written on the Wind.* Unlike the texts on which much of the theory of film melodrama has been constructed, *Dallas, Dynasty,* and their imitators lack the element considered crucial to theories of textual deficiencies that run counter to the dominant ideology—that is to say, they lack closure.

It would be misleading to discuss clotural conventions as excessive without considering their relationship to narrative/dramatic structure. For, as we have seen, moments of melodramatic excess relate to the serial structure of these dramas and occur as a form of temporary closure within and between episodes and even entire seasons. It is serial form, even more than visual conventions, which most distinguishes the contemporary television melodrama from its cinematic predecessors. And it is over the issue of serial form that arguments similar to the Brechtian position on Sirk have been proposed in theories of daytime serials.

A concept of closure is crucial to an argument that the "happy endings" in Sirk's films fail to contain their narrative excess, allowing contradictions in the text to remain exposed. According to several articles on this subject, the contradictions seemingly burst through the weakly knit textual seams, rendering closure ineffective. In this view a successful closure of the narrative would be seen as ideologically complicit with a smug, petit bourgeois view of the world. However the Sirk melodramas question that world view by leaving contradictions unresolved (see, for example, Orr 1980).

What becomes of this argument, though, when the representational field of melodrama takes the form of a serial drama that has no real beginning or end but only (as one critic describes it) "an indefinitely expandable middle" (Porter 1977, p. 783)? Since serials offer only temporary resolutions, it could be argued that the teleological metaphysics of classical narrative structure have been subverted. The moral universe of the prime-time serials is one in which the good can never ultimately receive their just rewards, yet evil can never wholly triumph. Any ultimate resolution—for good or for ill—goes against the only moral imperative of the continuing serial form; the plot must go on. It is not that *Dallas* and *Dynasty* lack the hermeneutic code. Quite the contrary, they contain an excess of plot in Brooks's sense of the term "melodrama." Continuing TV serials possess a strong drive toward resolution and do resolve most story lines. What differentiates an ongoing soap opera from a two-hour movie is that these moments of resolution are experienced in a very different way from the closure of a classical narrative film. Compare, for example, the ending of *Written on the Wind* to the 1986 season finale of *Dynasty*. When, at the end of the Sirk film, Rock Hudson and Lauren Bacall drive off together, the meaning is ambiguous because too much has been exposed to allow us to believe they will live simply and happily ever after. Yet, any speculation about the future life of the characters that a viewer might indulge in is just that, speculation. When on the other hand, Alexis occupies the Carrington mansion, we know that her moment of triumph can only be temporary. It is no accident that cliffhangers on daytime soaps and season finales of prime-time soaps tend to take place at weddings. As Lauren Rabinowitz points out, weddings form an exception to the rule that serials are merely endlessly flowing narratives without any kind of resolution. In fact, weddings are special events, increasingly announced and publicized in advance, and likely to occur during ratings sweeps (Rabinovitz 1992, pp. 277–278).

Yet in the serial, marriage—with its consequent integration into the social order—is never viewed as a symbol of narrative closure as it is in so many comic forms. Indeed to be happily married in a serial is to be on the periphery of the narrative. There are moments of equilibrium and even joy on TV serials, but in general we know that every happy marriage is eventually headed for divorce and that the very existence of the continuing serial rests on the premise that "all my children" cannot be happy at once (see Modleski 1982, p. 90). Thus the fate of various couples depends not on any fixed and eternal character traits (such as good/evil, happy/sad), but rather on a curious fulcrum principle in relationship to other couples in the current plot line. Characters who represent the societal good of happy monogamy with a desire to procreate are just as miserable as the fornicators. During the 1982–1983 season, the two marriages that seemed above the vagaries of intrigue—those of Pamela and Bobby Ewing, and Blake and Krystle Carrington—were torn asunder by obviously contrived plot devices. Even the implicit moral goodness of a character such as Pamela was called into question. In the plutocracies of *Dallas* and *Dynasty*, as in the more bourgeois worlds of daytime soaps, happy marriage does not make for interesting plot complications.

From this it might be argued that prime-time family dynasty serials in particular offer a criticism of the institution of bourgeois marriage, since marital happiness is never shown as a final state. Wedded bliss is desirable but also unobtainable. Moreover, that cornerstone of bourgeois morality—marriage for love—also appears to be demystified. Both *Dallas* and *Dynasty* deal with the economics of multinational corporations, but they do so in terms of the familial conflicts that control the destinies of these companies. This is typical of the domestic melodrama's oft-noted tendency to portray all ideological conflicts in terms of the family. However, *Dallas* and *Dynasty* also depict the family in economic terms, thus apparently demystifying the middle-class notion of marriage based on romantic love (e.g., J.R.'s remarrying of Sue Ellen in order to regain control of his son and heir or the Byzantine interweavings of the Colby and Carrington empires in *Dynasty*). In one episode of *Dynasty*, Blake Carrington buys his wife, Krystle, a new Rolls Royce, telling her that he is giving her the Rolls because she is giving him a child. This act would seem to reduce their love to a financial con-

tract, thus exposing its material basis. Yet in a sense these characters are beyond bourgeois morality because they represent the ruling class. Critic Michael Pollan has offered the interpretation that the transgressions of the nouveau riche decadents of prime time ultimately serve to reinforce bourgeois norms:

> *Dallas, Dynasty* and *Falcon Crest* give us the satisfaction of feeling superior to them: we can look down on their skewed values and perverted family lives from the high ground of middle-class respectability. When Angela Chaning (*Falcon Crest*) coolly threatens to disinherit her grandson if he won't wed a woman he despises (the marriage would tighten her hold on the valley's wine industry), our own superior respect for love and marriage is confirmed. The prime-time soaps also confirm the suspicion that great wealth and power are predicated on sin, and, even more satisfying, don't buy happiness anyway. (1982, pp. 14–15)

How can the same programs yield up such diametrically opposed readings? According to two feminist studies (Modleski 1982; Seiter 1982), serial form and multiple plot structure appear to give TV melodrama a greater potential for multiple and aberrant readings than do other forms of popular narrative. Since no action is irreversible, every ideological position may be countered by its opposite. Thus the family dynasty saga may be read either as critical of the dominant ideology of the Reagan era or as complicit with it, depending on the position from which the reader comes at it.

Of course most U.S. television programs are structured to appeal to a broad mass audience and to avoid offending any segment of that audience. The openness of TV texts does not in and of itself represent a politically progressive stance. Nevertheless, I would argue that the continuing melodramatic serial seems to offer an especially active role for the spectator, even in comparison to the previous decade's form-in-dominance, the socially conscious situation comedy of the early to mid-1970s. The popular press bemoaned the transition from these "quality" sitcoms to "mindless" comedies and "escapist" serials later in the decade. The popular sitcoms of the 1970s—for example, Norman Lear's *All in the Family* and *Maude,* and MTM Enterprises' *The Mary Tyler Moore Show* and *Rhoda*—were engaged with their times, often to the point of encompassing overtly political themes with a progressive bent. *Dallas* and *Dynasty* seem by contrast to be conservative Republican programs. The article by Michael Pollan goes on to argue that prime-time soaps duplicate the imagery of Reaganism and reinforce its ideology.

Although the sitcoms contained overtly liberal messages, their strong drive toward narrative closure tended to mask contradictions and force a false sense of social integration by the end of each episode. For example, the problems raised by *All in the Family* had to have easy solutions within the family so that a new topical issue could be introduced in the next episode. TV critic Michael J. Arlen has described this phenomenon very well in his essay "The Media Dramas of Norman Lear": "Modern, psychiatrically inspired or induced ambivalence may, indeed, be the key dramatic principle behind this new genre of popular entertainment. A step is taken, and then a step back. A gesture is made and then withdrawn—blurred into distracting laughter, or somehow forgotten. This seems especially true in the area of topicality" (Arlen 1974, p. 59). This does not mean that the sitcom form is incapable of expressing ambiguity. As Alexander Nehamas has pointed out, *All in the Family* frequently ended on a close-up of a character poised on the edge of an ideological contradiction. The issues posed are thus seen as pointing to irresolvable social contradictions (Nehamas 1990, p. 176–177). Yet, the following week, the ideological complication would not be reintroduced or complicated. Rather, the episodic series form demands that a new dilemma be introduced the following week. That is why the episodic series sitcom, however radical its content, lends itself so well to syndication schedules oblivious to the original chronology of the show. Thus the closure of a such a sitcom is more like the ambiguous ending of *Written on the Wind* than it is like serial melodrama. In the eighties, the materials of domestic melodrama almost always sought out serial form for their expression. Or rather, we could say that, unlike in the 1950s, melodrama and serial form were almost always articulated together, whereas the episodic series was reserved for comedy. Just as the made-for-TV trauma dramas could "swing both ways," the simple binary form of the sitcom could accommodate the ideological oppositions of both *All in the Family* and *Family Ties*, sitcoms whose structural similarities are obscured by their political differences. Both based their structure of ideological oppositions on generational differences between parents and their children, although with inverted values: the 1970s sitcom featured hippie children and reactionary parents; the 1980s sitcom, aging hippie parents and a neoconservative, aspiring-yuppie son. Originally, the latter show was fairly balanced between the parents' and the son's politics, but the success of Michael J. Fox in the role of Alex Keaton caused the sitcom's ideological balance to shift toward the Reaganite side. It is no accident, I believe, that after his success in the sitcom form, Norman Lear's subsequent venture into social satire took the form of the continuing serial *Mary Hartman, Mary Hartman* (1976), nor that both *Mary Hartman* and *Soap* (1977) blended situation comedy with elements of melodrama. It was not so much a question of resolving social contradictions as it was of finding a narrative structure that would give these contradictions greater force and play.

Nor could prime-time melodramas resolve contradictions by containing them within the family, since in this serialized form the family is the very site of ideological conflict and capitalist investment. Thus the corporate family becomes the overdetermined signifier of contradictions that will unravel in serial form but never find a permanent solution. Take, for example, the heated issue of Stephen Carrington and his vexed relationship with his father, Blake, a serial story line that was introduced in the first three episodes of *Dynasty*. Having a continuing homosexual character on a prime-time TV show was often touted by the producers as a sign of the show's liberalism on social issues. Indeed Stephen's gayness provided the narrative impetus for the first-season cliffhanger — Blake's trial for the murder of Stephen's lover — which in turn provided for the arrival of Alexis on the scene at the climax of the first season. Subsequently, Stephen went in and out of the closet. Just as his gayness remained unfixed, so his relationship with Blake oscillated from year to year (and even from Stephen to Stephen: the original actor — who returned to the role for the reunion miniseries — was much more visually coded as gay than was his replacement). When, for example, Blake Carrington reconciled with his homosexual son during Stephen's marriages to Claudia or to Sammy Jo, it did not represent an easy resolution to the challenge Stephen's gayness posed to the disposal of the Carrington fortune. The temporary reconciliations merely forecast yet another breach between father and son, which ensued when Stephen took his son and moved in with one or another of his male lovers, lovers easily disposed of in Moldavian terrorist attacks and other vagaries of plot.

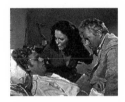

That this state of flux renders Stephen's gayness a matter of constant crisis is apparent when compared to the easy liberal acceptance of Stephen exhibited by Blake in *Dynasty: The Reunion* (1991). Thirty minutes into the four-hour miniseries, Blake is released from prison and goes to stay with Stephen. We find the gay son comfortably ensconced in a minimalist postmodern loft with gleaming hardwood floors with his partner, Bart, the gay son of the politician who figured in a scandalous revelation in the series proper. Yet the anticipated father-son confrontation over this settled homosexual lifestyle never en-

sues. Blake and son adjourn to a yuppie diner, where the following conversation takes place:

> *Blake:* Do you love each other?
>
> *Stephen:* Yes, we do.
>
> *Blake:* I envy you, Stephen. I wish I had Krystle with me now the way you have Bart. [They embrace.]

Why does the reunion miniseries dispense so easily with an ideological and familial conflict that had driven the serial's narrative since its inception? It does not seem to me that this can be explained entirely by situating the reunion as a post-Reagan retrospective event. Certainly one can read it as the producers' nod to their always loyal gay audience at a moment when they no longer have to worry about keeping the heterosexual mass audience. But I prefer to read the easy reconciliation of Blake and Stephen in terms of the differing imperatives of serial and end-oriented narrative forms. The entire purpose of *Dynasty: The Reunion* is closure; it was designed to tie together all of the narrative strands left unfinished when the series broadcast its last episode on 11 May 1989. In this regard, the *Dynasty* reunion is structurally more like the seventies liberal sitcom or *Written on the Wind* than it is like the serialized parent show. The forced integration of social contradictions leads to conclusions far more ideologically stabilizing even than those of the 1950s melodramatic film. Thus, unlike the earlier season cliffhangers that stressed the continuing threats posed by Alexis, the last scenes of the reunion find the Carringtons *en famille* at the corporate family table with even Alexis having been reconciled to familial and ideological harmony. If the *Dynasty* miniseries had not occurred, I would have needed to invent it to make my point about the different experience of resolution in the dominant popular narrative forms of the fifties, seventies, and eighties, respectively.

For different reasons a number of analysts have wanted to describe the change from sitcom to serial as the dominant narrative form of the seventies and eighties, respectively, as "progressive." However, all (including myself) have tended to confuse a narrative sense of "progress" with a political sense of the term. For the industry and the popular press that perpetuates its views, serials are progressive in that they affirm bourgeois notions of character development and growth. We can reject this explanation at two levels. First, it is arguable that a static conception of character is a more damning description of bourgeois social relations. Second, it is not correct to say that characters change in prime-time continuing serials. More often they perpetuate the narrative by continuing to make the same mistakes. Rather, owing to the multiple plot structure, characters' positions shift in relation to other characters. To quote Rick Altman, *"Dallas* is organised not according to a novelistic hermeneutic, but around an intricate menu of topics which for some viewers are experienced by character and for others by theme" (1987, p. 577). The diachronic development of continuing serials depends more on the shifting status of the various couples and families. At any given synchronic moment, families that were once integrated are now disintegrated, and vice versa. Integration into a happy family remains the ultimate goal, but it cannot endure for any given couple. The various sets of couples achieve in fulcrum fashion a balance between harmony and disharmony, but no one couple can remain in a state of integration (or of disintegration).

Audience studies of the 1970s sitcom make clear that "misreadings" are eminently possible; indeed the "liberal" structure of the Lear sitcom ensured differential readings of Archie's racism. However, I would still maintain that the emphasis on reintegration of the family does not allow as much space for a critique of the nuclear family structure itself.

For the continuing serial, the very need to "rupture" the family in order for the plot to continue can be viewed as a dangerous strategy in the sense that it allows for a reading of the disintegration as a critique of the family itself. Specifically, it threatens to explode the strategy of containment common to both the episodic series and the continuing serial by which all conflicts are expressed in terms of the family. In the sitcom, the threatening forces are reexpelled each week. The continuing serial, by contrast, maintains its "outside" within the family structure. The outside forces that threaten the sitcom family become the inside forces that threaten the internal disintegration of the continuing serial family. In allowing the family to be perennially torn apart, there is always the danger that the outside will explode upon the inside. We cannot, however, guarantee that this will lead to *politically* progressive readings of continuing serials. Rather than set up an opposition between the series and the serial along reactionary/radical lines, I would prefer to view them as two different responses to television's dual ideological compulsions: the need to repeat and the need to contain.

To put it schematically, the 1970s sitcoms dealt with liberal messages within a narrative form (the episodic series sitcom) limited by its own conservatism. The prime-time serials reverse this, bearing what appears to be a right-wing ideology by means of a potentially progressive narrative form. There is a parallel here to the populism of the made-for-TV movies discussed earlier, a populism whose inflection to the right rather than toward a socialistic reading depended on numerous factors outside the formal constraints of the films themselves. Narrative forms cannot in themselves structure the ideologies of an era, yet narrative forms—especially the very simple one of the TV sitcom—do have expressive limitations, and, in the case at hand, one can correlate a shift in the dominant narrative form of American network television with a shift in sensibilities outside the text. It would seem that the multiplication of social contradictions in the 1980s could not be expressed within the boundaries of the situation comedy. This is not to say, as many have argued, that the new serials represent a turning away from social concerns. The emergence of the melodramatic serial in the 1980s represents a *radical* response to and expression of cultural contradictions. Whether that response is interpreted to the right or to the left is not a question the texts themselves can answer. Indeed it is unlikely that a complex phenomenon such as *Dynasty* could be articulated in such conventional political terms. Instead one must examine the intricate and concrete circumstances of reception of a program such as *Dynasty* by audiences during the period of its greatest popularity: the mid-eighties, the peak of the Reagan era.

This is what the next chapter sets out to do. In exploring the way audiences might have responded to the forms and ideologies addressed in this chapter, one can discover compelling evidence that, at least for some audience groups, the Brechtian reading strategy was indeed pursued. In fact, the very excessive elements that authorize readings of *Dynasty* as a Brechtian text—camp, hysteria, fashion, floral arrangments, cat fights, and so forth—are the same elements that link *Dynasty* to the structure of feeling of the gay male urban subculture that fetishized the program.

Notes

1 Most of us who take daytime soaps seriously wouldn't buy this claim. Indeed in-house daytime audience research shows that female viewers possess a much greater interest in character than in plot. And prime-time soaps like *Dynasty* and *Melrose Place* have ten times the plot content of daytime soaps.

2 *Mary Hartman, Mary Hartman* (Syndicated, 1976–1977) and *Soap* (ABC, 1977–1981) mixed melodrama with comedy and parody.

3 Prime-time serial melodramas attempted during the eighties include *Bare Essence* (NBC, 1983), *Behind the Screen* (CBS, 1981–1982), *Berrenger's* (NBC, 1985), *The Colbys* (ABC, 1985–1987), *Emerald Point, N.A.S.* (CBS, 1983–1984), *Flamingo Road* (NBC, 1981–1982), *The Hamptons* (ABC, 1983), *King's Crossing* (ABC, 1982), *A New Day in*

Eden (Showtime, 1982–1983), *Paper Dolls* (ABC, 1984), *Rituals*, (Syndication, 1984–1985), *Secrets of Midland Heights* (1980–1981), and *The Yellow Rose* (1983–1984).

4 I wrote this before the Heather Locklear invasion of Melrose Place. I am letting it stand because I think that despite its many affinities to *Dynasty*, *Melrose Place* during the fabulous 1993–1994 season did not signify an historical period and Zeitgeist so much as it did a generational awareness (Generation X, twentysome-things, and this despite its wide appeal). In this sense, despite my love for the show, I would have to say that *Melrose* is no *Dynasty*. It is, however, the only nineties show truly to understand *Dynasty*'s contribution to the form of the melodramatic serial.

5 I discuss this critical trajectory at length in Feuer 1984.

6 As Landy notes, "One of Gramsci's major contributions to an understanding of political change is his emphasis on the importance of intellectuals as playing a significant role in the legitimation of power. In fact, for Gramsci, the study of intellectuals and their production is synonymous with the study of political power" (1986, p. 53).

6

The Reception of *Dynasty*

For a moment in the mid-1980s the television serial *Dynasty* ceased being merely a program and took on the proportions of a major mass cultural cult. This phenomenon has been widely interpreted as representing the acquiescence of the mass audience to the Reaganite ideology of greed and asocial avarice. But the response of the so-called masses to *Dynasty* was far more complex than a mere affirmation of the worst of Reaganism. This chapter will analyze the response to *Dynasty* as a complex phenomenon that has aspects of both commodification from above and subcultural activation from below.[1] For although *Dynasty* was the number one rated program overall in the 1984–1985 TV season, its fans were not simply a mass audience, but rather were clustered in two quadrants of a male/female, gay/straight *combinatoire*—that is to say, the two groups that became obsessed with *Dynasty* in the mid-1980s were gay men and heterosexual women. These are, precisely, the two groups most connected to commodified beauty culture, to notions of femininity as a commodity to be purchased. They are also groups that have been considered to possess distinct "subcultural" identities vis-à-vis a dominant straight white male culture. In the case of gay men, the subcultural identity depends on their outsider status to the patriarchal family; in the case of women, radical feminist thinking has stressed the extent to which all women constitute a separate culture or subculture within patriarchal society.

Thus it seems significant that neither lesbians nor straight men as a group were especially caught up in the *Dynasty* craze. Lesbian culture, constructed in many ways to expose or resist commodified femininity, in this case emerges as the diametric opposite to the gay male culture that fetishized *Dynasty*. Similarly, although individual heterosexual men no doubt watched the program, it did not attempt to create the kind of masculine identification epitomized by J.R. Ewing of *Dallas*. *Dynasty*'s dominating images of the bitchy "drag queen" Alexis, the wooden, aging Blake Carrington, and their tortured gay son Stephen, living in various combinations in overdecorated baroque mansions and postmodern penthouse apartments, meant that its links to male action-adventure programming were far more tenuous than those of *Dallas* with its suburban ranch-house mansion, cowboy husbands, and wimpy wives. *Dallas* also lacked the camp undercurrent that propelled *Dynasty* to the center of gay male culture during the mid-1980s. Yet it was these same elements that made *Dynasty* a hit in mainstream women's culture as well. According to Stephen Schiff, "Dynasty represents something extraordinary: the incursion of so-called gay taste into the mainstream of American Culture" (1984, p. 64).

Gay Activations

Within the gay male urban subculture, *Dynasty* functioned more as a ritual than as a text; it was enacted rather than consumed. According to Stephen Schiff, "*Dynasty* night is an inviolable ritual in gay bars across the country; at one in Los Angeles, tapes of epic catfights between Alexis and Krystle are played over and over on an endless loop. A ritual known as D. & D.—Dinner and *Dynasty*—has become a fixture of gay social life" (Schiff 1984, p. 64). *Dynasty*'s popularity with gay men was not primarily because of the liberal portrayal of Stephen as a "manly" homosexual, but rather because of its camp attitude embodied especially in the figure of Alexis, who Schiff describes as a "perfect bitch" and "the apotheosis of the camp aesthetic" (p. 66). As Mark Finch reports, "The Hippodrome club (gay for one night each week) held a *Dallas* and *Dynasty* ball on 16 July 1984, with over sixty look-alike contestants, mostly dressed as Alexis" (Finch 1986, p. 37).

Although camp is not entirely a property of texts but rather comes into being when an audience interacts with a text, not just any text can be camped, and *Dynasty* certainly facilitates the process with its penchant for excess. If there were ever a moment prior to the camp activations by the mainstream audience, that moment preceded *Dynasty*'s popularity.

Even during the exploratory first season, Pamela Sue Martin as Fallon occupied the space of excess that Alexis would later take over. At the wedding of Blake and Krystle that opened the series, we see Fallon mounting the baronial staircase of the mansion, biting off the heads of the bride and groom figurines from the massive wedding cake. Very early on, the show's producers were aware of the show's excesses and intended to encode them in the text by devising "outrageous plots" and

"walk[ing] a fine line, just this side of camp" (Klein 1985, p. 34). Evidence exists that both urban gay men and middle-class straight women were enacting camp readings of *Dynasty* from a very early stage; these two very different "interpretive communities" were reading *Dynasty* in a similar way.

In what sense were gay men and middle-class heterosexual women "interpretive communities" for *Dynasty*? The term comes from Stanley Fish's literary theory, but contemporary literary interpretive communities differ greatly from those for mass-mediated culture in the sense that the former's raison d'être is reading . They are, that is to say, groups of professional interpreters. Television reception theorists have always assumed that popular audiences are already socially constituted; as Bennett and Woollacott (1987) put it, the "inter-textually" constituted reader meets the "intertextually" constituted text.[2] This is another way of saying that neither the text nor the community should be given priority when theorizing the constitution of popular subjectivity through encounters by subcultures with mass-mediated texts. Stanley Fish has been criticized from within literary studies for failing to recognize that "interpretive communities are bound to be communities on other grounds as well, bound to have common interests besides the production of interpretations, bound to correspond to other social differentiations" (Pratt 1986, p. 52).

This critique is even more valid when discussing interpretive communities for television programs. The gay community is certainly a community based on grounds other than the interpretation of artistic texts, although it is that as well. And, through the acting out of a process of commodification, heterosexual American women become an interpretive community as well united in a least common denominator devotion to the culture of femininity.[3]

In literary reception theory, the notion of the reader "activating" the text has to do with cognitive processes rather than any kind of motor activity. But in activating *Dynasty*, the text becomes an event and even, in some cases, a way of life. At a time when urban gay men had reason to fear for their own lives, Schiff reported that fans in the East Village gay community "don't talk about [*Dynasty*] as if it were their favorite program. They talk about it as if it were their life" (1984). As we shall see, from the perspective of the producers as well, the Carrington lifestyle is offered as something to be achieved rather than merely interpreted. Although I cannot think of a single instance in which I was encouraged to smell a literary text, advertising for the fragrances Forever Krystle and Carrington offer up the odor of great romance in a quite literal way by including "scent strips" with the print ads. When the product insert exhorts me "to experience the love that lives forever . . . rub center fold along your pulse points," the gap between fantasy and fulfillment appears narrow indeed. *Dynasty* as event provides the perfect example of the pleasure to be obtained from being commodified.

Dynasty as Event

Dynasty Night parties have started to spring up all over the country in night clubs and supper houses. When I was in Hawaii in April, I found a club which built its entire Wednesday night around the show, even though *Dynasty* is seen a week behind the mainland's showing. And in Los Angeles, one such club shows first the previous week's episode, and then the current episode. The marked difference is the fact that the audience is very vocal about the proceedings. Every time ALI MACGRAW (Ashley) came on the screen she would be hissed like a villain, which she is, of course, not. JOAN COLLINS (Alexis) is received with cheers, not only when she appears in the opening credits, but every time she appears in a new NOLAN MILLER creation. LINDA EVANS (Krystle) is mildly received, but her dark-haired character, friend of Sammy Jo (HEATHER LOCKLEAR), is literally laughed at. The clientele is mostly male and at times the dialogue is difficult to hear because of remarks, often very funny, made about what is happening on the two giant screens. (Rizzo 1985, p. 37)

This text from *Soap Opera Digest* represents a report on *Dynasty* as an event while at the same time belonging to the *Dynasty* event. It also represents an interpretation of *Dynasty* from within a popular critical apparatus. Our critic (the esteemed Tony Rizzo) appears to be a disciple of E. D. Hirsch in his slavish adherence to the idea of textual determinacy. Therefore he is not a very astute analyst of the fascinating and complex phenomenon of reading on which he reports in our text. His reading assumes a morally stable reading formation implied by traditional conceptions of melodrama.[4] It also assumes that the critic's own reading of the program (that is, his attribution of good and evil labels to the characters) is a correct reading of the text, against which the reading by a very different interpretive community (that is, as his subtext implies, the gay male community) is seen as aberrant or, at the very least, a distortion of the true meaning of the text. Rizzo thus appears puzzled that two of the "good" characters are greeted with laughter, while the villainess of the melodrama (and her wardrobe) are greeted with cheers. But of course this reading disregards the very nature of a "camp" decoding, which is usually an "oppositional" one if only because it is made from a social position outside of dominant social values. Here the criteria being applied are aesthetic rather than moral, the standards of a community for whom aesthetics and morality are not mutually opposed categories of thought. Lady Ashley is not an evil character; rather, Ali MacGraw is a terrible actress—not just a regular "bad actress," for everyone on *Dynasty* is that, but a bad camp actress. (Joan Collins, on the other hand is a brilliant camp actress.) By looking at the entire reading formation, rather than centering on a reading of a text, this becomes obvious.

Dynasty's becoming an event was not entirely imposed from above; there is a great deal of evidence to consider it a type of subcultural appropriation of a text. In fact a study of the various activations of *Dynasty* makes clear the idea that the process of commodification is an interactive one, neither entirely spontaneously generated from below nor imposed from above—rather a dialectical interplay of each. The passage from *Soap Opera Digest* describes an actual subcultural activation in its portrayal of camp decodings. It is important to stress that the camp attitude toward *Dynasty* in both gay and mainstream culture does not preclude emotional identification; rather it embraces both identification and parody—attitudes normally viewed as mutually exclusive—at the same time and as part of the same sensibility. As Richard Dyer has written, the gay sensibility "holds together qualities that are elsewhere felt as antithetical: theatricality and authenticity . . .

'Dynasty': Is the thrill gone?

By Matt Roush
USA TODAY

Dynasty's creators tonight unveil a second weekly hour of prime-time suds — just as many fans are grumbling they've had enough.

Last year, Dynasty finished No. 1 for the season. This week, it was fifth in the Nielsen weekly ratings.

Lynda Hirsch, the nationally syndicated soap opera columnist, says she's received about 300 letters from fans complaining, "Why is Dynasty so bad this season?"

But Hirsch, who says, "No one's running home to turn it on," adds she heard from people who thought last week's show was the best Dynasty episode yet. "I think they're intrigued by the spinoff." Last week's show introduced many characters and plots of the new spinoff, The Colbys, premiering on ABC tonight at 10 EST/PST.

Hirsch says viewers have complained about the disappointing resolution to last season's cliffhanger, in which the stars were caught in a terrorist crossfire at a wedding. "People tuned in (this year) and saw a joke — everybody streaming out of the church yelling at the terrorists."

Esther Shapiro, a Dynasty creator and an executive producer, blames ABC for not wanting to show the bloodied images from inside the chapel.

■ Spinoff's premier, 1D
■ Review, family tree, 2D

'Dynasty' trouble
Viewers were asked how they enjoy Dynasty this year compared with last:

More	21%
Less	34%
Same	45%

Source: USA TODAY poll of 1,217 men and women; 32 percent watch program

USA TODAY

---

intensity and irony, a fierce assertion of extreme feeling with a deprecating sense of its absurdity" (1986, p. 154). In a similar vein, Andrea Press has noted that a representative middle-class woman she interviewed, while overtly belittling the show as ridiculous, actually "display[ed] an involvement with the show which belies this detached account of her interest in it" (1990, p. 174).

On the evening of the fall 1985 season premiere that would reveal the outcome of the previous season's cliffhanger (the Moldavian massacre), the lead story on the ABC-affiliate evening news in my local market concerned the way in which "local citizens" had gathered to celebrate this event. Nothing illustrates the camp sensibility toward *Dynasty* better than the news clip reporting on these *Dynasty* parties. The camp attitude is apparent both in the style of the report and in its content. On the one hand, the *Dynasty* craze is taken seriously enough to justify its being the lead story on the eleven o'clock news; on the other hand, the station has to indicate that it does not really take the phenomenon seriously. In this way both the fans and the reporter are camping; the reporter through a tongue-in-cheek tone, the fans through their energetic but inevitably failed attempts to provide a simulacrum of the Carringtons' lifestyle.

Over shots of fans arriving at the Hyatt Hotel in evening clothes, the *Dynasty* theme is playing. But something is not quite right. The evening clothes are makeshift and one young man is sipping champagne in a crew neck sweater. The narration is ironic: "They came looking as dashing as Blake Carrington, as daring as Alexis and everyone seemed to enjoy playing their chosen roles." When the re-

porter switches to another *Dynasty* party—this time at a singles bar—
the revelers seem to be camping for the cameras: a young woman with
a rhinestone tiara and long white gloves toasts us self-consciously. Perhaps the most ironic costume is that of another young woman mas-
querading in camouflage as a Moldavian terrorist and bearing plastic
arms. On the one hand, these fans were willing to go to extremes; on
the other hand, they are unwilling to admit to the cameras that they are
intensely emotionally involved—whether in the program itself or in
the camp event. And yet their attitude is remarkably similar to that of
the audience in Hawaii. All are especially scornful toward Ali MacGraw
(Lady Ashley). As one fan tells the reporter, "The big news is that Lady
Ashley is dead, Ali MacGraw no more." And an older woman reports
that "every kid in the office chose Lady Ashley to die." When, at the end
of the report, the reporter does a sarcastic yet detailed stand-up on the
outcome of the Moldavian massacre, the circuit of camp simulation is
completed.

Contrasting with these "subcultural" displays were attempts "from
above" to impose *Dynasty* upon us. Foremost among these was a practice of interweaving advertising with programming segments on *Dynasty* and *The Colbys*. Historians of advertising and of the soap opera
have emphasized the idea of the "interwoven commercial." According
to Roland Marchand, the advertising community initially believed that
the radio audience would not accept direct advertising, since it would
represent an intrusion into the family circle. It was felt that advertising
that was interwoven into the very fabric of the program would appear
more subtle and thus less jarring to the sensibilities of the listener (1985,
pp. 89–110). Robert Allen has shown the extent to which radio soap operas diegetically interwove advertising and programming (1985, pp.
151). Although for many years the U.S. networks moved away from
these practices, they are now returning to them because advertisers fear
the dreaded postmodern practice of "zapping," rapidly changing channels whenever an ad appears. Thus, on MTV the commercials are often
virtually indistinguishable from the videos.

Dynasty, as a fully commodified text, also returns us to these practices. Many of the ads, particularly those directly following a program
segment, are for perfume and other cosmetic products; they reproduce
the opulent mise-en-scène of the Carrington mansion and Alexis's
postmodern penthouse. But two ads in particular relate directly to the
program "text." These are usually shown between the end of the
episode and the previews, and they feature Krystle Carrington herself—or is it Linda Evans? We're not sure. The ads for Ultress and For-

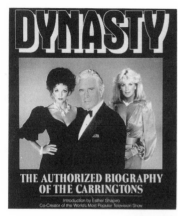

ever Krystle are so closely linked to the mise-en-scène and narrative of the parent program that only a knowledge of the conventions of television flow permit us to distinguish them. In the Forever Krystle/Carrington ad, Krystle and Blake play themselves, in *Dynasty*-like settings. Taking the form of a thirty-second epistolary novel, the couple are shown corresponding about the fragrances they have just had especially created for each other. A printed title at the end shows the perfume logos with the superimposed words "for the love that lives forever." There is no implication that these products are for sale at your corner drugstore; indeed it is implied that millions have been spent in order that these scents be unique to Blake and Krystle. In order to identify with the ad, the viewer has to take up the position of the Carringtons and identify with this exclusive luxury. No wonder this ad was frequently camped, for in camping it, the economic sleight of hand behind it is exposed—"I've had this fragrance created especially for anyone who wants to walk in and buy it" is hardly a message for the Reagan era. The scents must trickle down to all of us.

The Ultress commercials (there were ultimately three versions) are a little harder to read as direct reflections of the show's narrative. Such a reading of the earliest one might go as follows: To be sure there is

Krystle, walking down the sweeping staircase of a somewhat bour-geoisified version of the Carrington mansion (perhaps she is visiting), talking to us about her hair and caressing the hair of various other women at the gathering. But who is the strange gentleman whose arm Krystle takes at the end of her stroll? And where is Blake? Even these questions may be accommodated to the typical discontinuities of the parent text. Perhaps another Daniel Reese has appeared on the scene? Will Krystle finally cheat on her husband? Does this account for the bounce in her walk and the shine in her hair? The second Ultress ad finds Krystle among a harem of beautiful women (all of whom color their hair) in some kind of baroque salon. It doesn't take much to imagine that she is at one of the many charity balls the Carringtons are wont to attend, perhaps even the one where they ran into Henry Kissinger.

And indeed the placement of these ads relies on the continuity pro-vided by flow in order to erase the boundaries of the different program segments. The imagery of the commercials was reinforced in print ads that ran in many glossy magazines. We can read these ads as contin-uous with the program, or we can read them as commentaries on the program. As part of the text of *Dynasty*, the ads for Ultress and Forever Krystle merely continue the development of the perfect relationship between Blake and Krystle, the "love that lives forever." Even the fact that Joan Collins went off on her own to endorse a cheaper perfume, Scoundrel, seems entirely in keeping with her Alexis-like narcissism.

And yet, the interwoven ads could also be read against the program, in that their contrast with the tone and mood of the show gives away their attempts to manipulate us. For the ads are exactly the wholly af-firmative endorsement of Reaganite ideology that the program as a whole has been accused of being. Historian Debora Silverman is inter-ested in *Dynasty* because the show seems to support her claim that Diana Vreeland's exhibits at both the Metropolitan Museum and Bloomingdale's are direct reflections of the aristocratic ideology of the 1980s. She notes "a mutually reinforcing connection between popular opulent fashion and the dual roles of White House Nancy Reagan on the one hand and the television fantasy of *Dynasty*'s Krystle Carrington on the other." She concludes that Reagan's remarkable success is de-pendent on tapping "*Dynasty* themes in ordinary Americans' imagina-tions" (Silverman 1986, pp. 152–155). But the analogy she notes is be-tween Nancy Reagan and Krystle Carrington, whereas it is Alexis in particular and the show as a whole that allow for the outlet of the same hostility that was directed at Nancy Reagan. Joan Collins's brilliant camp performance as Alexis permitted certain audiences to identify with her and against the entire Nancy/Krystle ideological complex even when the narrative level of the show encouraged us to identify against Alexis. The ads, in contrast, present a completely positive view of the rich and famous, a completely positive affirmation of the Carringtons as the perfect couple, echoing perhaps William F. Buckley's nauseating paen to the Reagans in the June 1985 issue of *Vanity Fair:* "People curious to know how it is between the man and wife dancing together on the cover of *Vanity Fair* this month are going to have to put to one side their political feelings and recognize that is the way they are" (quoted in Blumenthal 1988, p. 274). The only time the text proper sustained such an affirmation of the Carrington family dynasty as a whole and the Blake/Krystle marriage in particular is in the final scene of *Dynasty: The Reunion.* As the stiff, aging Carringtons slow dance (as if echoing Buckley), the camera pulls back on the unfurnished Carrington ballroom. As the *Dynasty* theme reaches a musical climax, so does the show. We are reminded that it is 1991 and the Reagans are no longer our first couple.

That is to say the ads and the final moments of the reunion completely miss the campy tone and delightful bitchiness of much of the show. Nor do the commercials capture the critical tone of the show, its foregrounding of the often violent power relations that underlay the Carringtons' "happy" marriage. Take, for instance, the contrast between the "Forever Krystle" commercial and the show proper. When Blake writes, "I had this fragrance created especially for you," he neglects to mention that most of the gifts he gave Krystle had strings attached—largely, reproductive ones. During the first season, Blake had flowers created especially for his new wife after raping her the night before because he discovered she was taking birth control pills. Similarly, Krystle's enabling of the Carrington scent for men in the ad neglects to mention that, at the time of the rape, she had just sold the emeralds from her hope chest to finance the oil wells of her former lover, Matthew Blaisdel, oil wells whose leases Blake was desperate to snare.

In this way advertising and program segments may jar rather than blend, especially at moments of supreme melodrama. *Dynasty*'s 21 May 1986 season finale was followed by the second Ultress ad. After listening to Alexis describe Krystle as a "blonde tramp" at the moment of her supreme victory over the couple (she has taken over Blake's entire fortune including his house), and after watching the aging Blake ludicrously try to strangle Alexis in a moment of total melodramatic excess, it is difficult to believe that merely possessing Linda Evans's hair color will elevate one into the lifestyles of the rich and famous. There is no question that for most of the audience the fascination was with the look of the Carringtons. But this does not mean that they read Blake and Krystle as the totally positive reincarnation of Ron and Nancy, as Debora Silverman seems to imply. The meaning of the desire to simulate the world of the Carringtons was far more complex than that.

The *Dynasty* Collection

This desire to simulate the world of the Carringtons was both a product of and an influence on the show's producers. As a 1985 *Cosmopolitan* article explains, "Appearances are important because if there is any single component that separates *Dynasty* from the rest of television, it is what everyone associated with the show—from executive producer Aaron Spelling on down—refers to as the look" (Warren 1985, pp. 182–185). The article goes on to describe—as do so many other reports in the popular press during this period—the extreme care the producers of *Dynasty* take with its "look": they worry about the jewelry matching, the colors of the clothes matching the mood, even the manner in which the dinner table settings are photographed (in detail with close-ups). As the article explains, "A huge cult following has developed around [Alexis's] gustatory habits. Interest is so great that several newspapers have been running contests for fans to guess what she'll put in her mouth next" (p. 185). Every detail is authentic: when Blake presented Krystle with a Rolls-Royce Corniche, the scene had to be reshot because the keys he handed her weren't standard Rolls keys.

Not only was *Dynasty* the only television program to have a resident fashion designer, it was the only program that thrust its costume designer into stardom. It is no accident that in the Tony Rizzo *Soap Opera Digest* column quoted above, the name of designer Nolan Miller figures as prominently as that of the show's major stars. *Dynasty* had a costume budget of $25,000 per episode with $100,000 allocated for the royal wedding that closed the 1984 season. According to the *Wall Street Journal,* Nolan Miller received over one hundred fan letters weekly in 1984 (1984, p. 1). No star could have a more devoted following, as evidenced by the following testimonial: "Your designs and styles overwhelm me, sometimes they actually take my breath away. . . . I usually miss each scene's first lines because I'm too busy studying each outfit" (*Wall Street Journal* 23 March 1984, p. 1).

When Nolan Miller appeared on the *Phil Donahue Show* with his collection of ready-to-wear garments based on the show, each outfit was greeted by near-delirious applause. He played the role of *auteur* to the hilt: "I'm responsible for *everything*." Since, as many commentators have pointed out, the program served as an hour-long commercial for the clothes, it was only a matter of time before a desire to possess the material objects of the Carrington lifestyle would emerge in the audience. Whereas the homemade simulacra exhibited at *Dynasty* parties could not profit the show's producers directly, the potential for mass-produced products based on the show might satisfy both voracious fans and the needs of capital. Hence was born the *Dynasty* Collection, whose products included lingerie, hosiery, shoes, blouses, suits, linens, sheets, china, glasswear, perfume, tuxedos, and even Alexis and Krystle porcelain dolls in Nolan Miller fashions (real mink stoles, real diamond necklaces) retailing for $10,000 apiece (*Los Angeles Times* 1985, p. 6). Previous programs had licensed commercial products tied in to their narratives, but the *Dynasty* Collection would be the first upscale product licensing geared to an adult public. *Dynasty*'s producers and their equivalents at Twentieth Century–Fox Licensing Corporation made endless claims that the *Dynasty* Collection had emerged in response to spontaneous audience requests for copies of the Carringtons' goods. *Dynasty* cocreator Esther Shapiro says: "People seem fascinated with the trappings. After one episode . . . we got 4,500 requests from women who wanted to know where to buy Joan Collins's suit" (*New York Times* 1984a, p. C29).

According to Chuck Ashman, president of Twentieth Century–Fox Licensing Corporation: "The idea for tie-ins came from those fanatical fans. The mail that comes in is as often directed to a dress as much as it is to a star." Esther Shapiro says she realized "people want to be part of it all, so it just seemed logical that we extend to merchandising" (*People* 1984, p. 69). Both Ashman and Shapiro felt the need to identify the merchandising campaign as coming from consumer demand rather than an attempt they themselves masterminded to cash in on the success of the show. The licensing corporation had reason to believe that *Dynasty* would be the perfect vehicle. Its demographics were superb—the number one rated show among women of all ages. According to Chuck Ashman, "In one informal survey 29 of 30 women stopped on Seventh Avenue admitted an addiction to the show—and confessed that they watched it largely for the clothes" (*New York* 1984, p. 15).

When the *Dynasty* Collection premiered at Bloomingdale's, over twenty thousand fans packed the store in order to view not just the collection but also some of the show's stars, who were there for the event. "We have not had such excitement in Bloomingdale's since the Queen of England visited in 1976," remarked chairman Marvin Traub. The *New York Times* goes on to describe one of the fans present: "She was wearing a blue T-shirt with '*Dynasty* addict' spelled out in rhinestones" (1984b, p. C15).

According to hypodermic or effects theories, the *Dynasty* merchandising campaign could not fail. And yet, although some of the less expensive products such as the perfumes were financial successes, it would appear that most of the collection did indeed fail to attract the fans. In 1986, the big-ticket items were taken off the market (*Wall Street Journal* 1986, p. 31). Apparently, *Dynasty*'s mass audience had the power to desire the items but not to purchase them. The ultimate financial failure of the *Dynasty* Collection raises interesting questions for a reception aesthetics that acknowledges the commodified nature of mass cultural decodings but that does not construct a binary opposition between commodification and subcultural activation. Perhaps the financial failure of the *Dynasty* Collection was also an ideological failure. No one wants to buy Nolan Miller ready-to-wear dresses—they want to act out the fantasy in thrift shop garb. In this case, the subcultural activation by gays and women defeats the commodification of the Fox Licensing Corporation—it becomes an act of resistance. This interpretation is very different from interpreting fan culture around *Dynasty* as mere modeling on greed and avarice—as a mere simulacrum of the Reagans.

In fact the *Dynasty* simulation mania may have stemmed at least in part from the same impetus as the general cultural hostility toward Nancy Reagan. For the flip side of Ronnie's popularity was always Nancy-baiting, a popular pastime among many who may have voted for Reagan. In Veblenesque fashion, she carried the burden of conspicuous consumption for them both. During the early Reagan presidency, "she was dubbed 'Queen Nancy,' said to be concerned above all with her new $200,000 White House china, interior decorators—and clothing designers—which of course, she was" (Blumenthal 1988, p. 272). Note that these were also the three things *Dynasty* was most interested in. Terry Sweeney's retrospective 1990 off-Broadway show *It's Still My Turn*, in which Sweeney delivered a brilliant drag impersonation of Mrs. Reagan, took the same campy attitude toward Nancy as did many of the gay camp simulations of *Dynasty*, portraying her in a red Adolpho suit as staggeringly indifferent to the suffering Reaganomics had caused.

Given all of this, in what sense do we want to call these activations of *Dynasty* "readings" in the literary sense? When we speak of a "reading" or "interpretation" of a literary text, we usually assume that we are referring to an attribution of meaning at a high level of abstraction—telling us what the text means. Reader-response theorists have taught us that there exists a far more basic sense of "reading" consisting of the attribution of meaning to the actual words on the page. But does even this basic level of meaning attribution occur when, in the "Nolan Miller" reading of *Dynasty*, viewers watch to see the clothes? And what kind of interpretive act is signified by attempts to replicate the material signifiers of the Carringtons in the lives of the audience?

Indeed the audience activation of *Dynasty* through ritualized events may represent a refusal of meaning attribution as a positive act and thus could be labeled "postmodern" in Baudrillard's sense. When Baudrillard speaks of the masses in relationship to meaning, he could be describing what the masses do with *Dynasty* (in a postmodern sense as opposed to one derived from subcultural theory):

> Thus, in the case of the media, traditional resistance consists of reinterpreting messages according to the group's own code and for its own ends. The masses, on the contrary, accept everything and redirect everything *en bloc* into the spectacular, without requiring any other code, without requiring any meaning, ultimately without resistance, but making everything slide into an indeterminate sphere which is not even that of non-sense, but that of overall manipulation/fascination. (1983a, pp. 43–44)

The activations of *Dynasty* could also be called postmodern in another sense, having to do with the relationship between the program and its simulators. The homemade Nolan Miller gowns, just as the commodified ones, might be considered a form of pastiche, what Fredric Jameson considers to be the postmodern form of parody. According to Jameson, pastiche is "blank parody" in an age when personal style is no longer there to be imitated. Hence it lacks the satirical or critical edge of modernist parody. It simply mimics the preexisting form (Jameson 1984). In its use of pastiche, then, the *Dynasty* reading formation is working within the postmodern era and in a postmodern style.

But ultimately neither of these senses of the postmodern captures the double-edged quality of Dyer's definition of the camp sensibility in which blank mimicry and a critical edge may coexist. That is to say, we are observing both subcultural appropriation and postmodern pastiche at the same time and from within the same sensibility. It is this double-edged quality, according to Linda Hutcheon, that distinguishes postmodern parody. Arguing against Jameson, she proposes that postmodern architecture is a contradictory enterprise when viewed from the perspective of its actual praxis. And parody, she believes, is one of its primary weapons, if we define parody as "repetition with critical distance that allows ironic signaling of difference at the very heart of similarity" (1986–1987, p. 185). In postmodern architecture, parody occurs from an inside position, and it is combined with a kind of historical reverence. Here Hutcheon quotes Charles Jencks's comment that the Venturis' desire to learn from Las Vegas expresses "a mixed appreciation for the American Way of Life. Grudging respect, not total acceptance. They don't share all the values of a consumer society, but they want to speak to this society, even if partially in dissent" (p. 194). Hutcheon's description of postmodern parody as setting up "a dialectical relationship between identification and distance" (p. 206) describes perfectly the camp sensibility toward *Dynasty*; it does not require an avant-garde sensibility to make a postmodern parody of *Dynasty*.

Yet it was not just imaginary "postfeminist" women and "apolitical" gay men who were fascinated by *Dynasty*. When a cadre of left-leaning media scholars set out to produce their own TV shows for public-access cable TV and "syndicate" them nationally in the form of a guerrilla network called Paper Tiger Television, the most popular program turned out to be *Joan Does Dynasty* (1986), a clever work of video art that preserved much of the double-edged, camp, playful, postmodern tone that characterized *Dynasty* and the mass cult that had formed around it. Joan Braderman quite literally inserts her body into scenes from the program, all the while delivering a running ironic commentary expressing her ambivalent attitude of fascination/repulsion toward *Dynasty*. The half-hour program represented Joan Braderman's bid to be included in the illustrious line of divas bearing the name of Joan: Crawford, Collins, and Rivers.[5] Yet the many examples of double-edged attitudes toward *Dynasty* discussed earlier make avant-garde activations of the text almost superfluous. In many respects, *Joan Does Dynasty* merely reproduces what many in the mass audience already "did" with *Dynasty*. Her "camp" activation is certainly postmodern, but no more so than wearing a blue T-shirt with "*Dynasty* addict" spelled out in rhinestones.

Of course we can also locate more traditional interpretations of *Dynasty* both in the popular media and in more academic publications.

These I call "ideological readings," because although they do attempt to spell out what *Dynasty* means, it is always in terms of the political Zeitgeist of the era and never in terms of any kind of close textual analysis or detailed ethnographic work. Several writers including Debora Silverman, quoted above, have remarked on the similarities between the Carringtons and the Reagans, noting that *Dynasty* began broadcasting a few weeks after the first Reagan inaugural in 1981. By January 1991, *Dynasty* producer Douglas Cramer was quoted as saying: "The Reagans are out of the White House, and John (Forsythe) and Joan (Collins) are out of the mansion. You only have to look at the papers to see where we are in terms of the recession and the homeless" (Zurawik 1991).

Interviews with the producers served to validate an awareness of the parallelism between the Reagans and the Carringtons. Although *Dynasty* began broadcasting a few weeks after the first Reagan inaugural in 1981, Esther Shapiro claims it was several years before she noticed the resemblances: "a powerful executive married to a devoted woman, with a difficult ex-wife, a sensitive son, a rebellious daughter . . . and beyond that, the idea that having money and flaunting it, enjoying it, is okay — they have that in common, too" (Klein 1985, p. 35). In "The Season of the Reagan Rich," Michael Pollan argues that TV shows about rich people thrived in the Reagan era precisely because the imagery of the Reagans and their TV analogues are mutually reinforcing ideologically:

> Like the millionaires who propelled Ronald Reagan into politics — Charles Z. Wick, Justin Dart, the late Alfred Bloomingdale — the rich of prime time are all self-made men who accumulated vast fortunes in the West. As Washington society noted sourly on its arrival, the Reagan crowd is hopelessly *nouveau riche*, deficient in the graces and decorum that distinguishes the older families of the East. . . . Television's rich and the Reagan rich also share something more insidious — their nostalgic fantasy of wealth in America. . . . Both imply that the American dream of self-made success is alive and might be made well by releasing the frontier instincts of the wealthy from the twin shackles of taxes and regulation. (Pollan 1982, pp. 14–15)

Arguably, there is a link between the postmodern readings and the ideological ones, since the ideological readings are presumably interpreting the postmodern activations. Silverman's agenda appears to be to "read" the reading formation of Reaganite cultural politics, which in turn have produced the shallow, aristocratic postmodern activations in the mass culture. Arguably this is not what she achieves, however, because she does not understand the subcultural aspects of the post-modern readings. The danger of an ideological reading is that it will proceed directly from thin description to condemnation. As Janice Radway has shown, it is only by seeing from the perspective of those inside of a reading formation that the true complexity of popular reading can be understood (1984). Ideological critics are attempting to fix *Dynasty*'s meaning, since any interpretation stabilizes the meaning of a text. However, these ideological readings tend to miss the camp activations, attributing to prime-time serials a parallelism of attitude as well as representational symbolism of Reaganomics. From this type of traditional ideological reading, it is easy to read off effects—always negative—on the viewer. Watching *Dynasty* must be bad for us, mustn't it? Thus Reaganism proves the dangerousness of *Dynasty*, while *Dynasty* proves the dangerousness of Reaganism in what Fredric Jameson has referred to as "billiard ball causality" (1981, p. 25). Looking at *Dynasty* from such a cultural perspective can only produce the type of ideological reading just described. It is only from the perspective of a postmodern concept of ideology that the subcultural activations of *Dynasty* can be understood in all of their multivalence and ambivalence.

Conclusion

A theory of reception for a mass cultural text must take into account the program's location within an intertextual network of commodity production. Thus *Dynasty*'s interpretive communities never merely interpret—they enact, they are counted as demographics, they consume not just a fictional text but a whole range of products as well. I would posit that the interpretive community not only *is* the text, it also *produces* the text and in addition is produced *by* the text. The postmodern reading formations described in this book were, arguably, producing a "dominant reading" of the program in the sense that many different contemporary interpretive communities approached the program from the postmodern perspective. But studying the camp sensibility that surrounded *Dynasty* within both gay and straight culture, and placing the program's reception within the entire circuit of commodity tie-ins calls into question the whole notion of a dominant reading as it is usually conceptualized by ideological criticism. For what is produced is not exactly a reading, and it is not exactly dominant either. Interpretive communities for *Dynasty* are not producing the same kind of interpretations as are interpretive communities for *Ulysses*. Seen in terms of reading formations, the activation of *Dynasty* is easily the more complex. Nor is the kind of ironic activation described—typical of the gay sensibility—exactly part of a "dominant ideology" that pervades American culture. It is something slippery and not easily transcodable into direct political and cultural effects. As a postmodern TV program, *Dynasty* challenges our received ideas about what an oppositional text might be and even of how opposition occurs in a seemingly hegemonic era.

Notes

1 Tony Bennett proposes the term "activation" as a means of "displacing . . . the concept of interpretation and the particular construction of relations between texts and readers that it implies" (Bennett 1983, p. 3).

2 Bennett and Woollacott define "inter-textuality" as follows: "Whereas Kristeva's concept of *intertextuality* refers to the system of references to other texts which can be discerned within the internal composition of a specific individual text, we intend the concept of *inter-textuality* to refer to the social organisation of the relations between texts within specific conditions of reading" (1987, pp. 44–45).

3 On another level, qualitative research suggests that women's interpretations of *Dynasty* may be divided along class lines as well as those of sexual preference. See Press 1990, pp. 158–180. Press found that working-class women were more likely to view the show as realistic, whereas middle-class women, while viewing it as fantasy, also tended to identify more with the characters.

4 Tony Bennett offers the following definition of a "reading formation": "a set of intersecting discourses that productively activate a given body of texts and the relations between them in a specific way" (1983, p. 5).

5 It is an enviable heritage; just contemplating it makes me want to alter a letter here and there.

Afterword: Overturning the Reagan Era

Although it would be foolish to propose a precise end date for the "Reagan era," there exist many candidates for this dubious signifying honor. Beginning with the 1987 stock market crash, one can move on to the end of the Reagan presidency, the cancellation of *Dynasty*, the airing of the *Dynasty* reunion miniseries, the election of Bill Clinton, or the *Time* magazine cover of 16 August 1993.

My personal favorite stylistic marker, however, is the decline and corporate takeover of *Metropolitan Home* magazine. In 1993, the magazine was taken over by a conglomerate, and we were told that the only new trend in home design is painting your walls yellow, and they started advertising Ethan Allen furniture. The new *Met Home* was reminiscent of the auctioning off of the Carringtons' antique treasures in favor of a suburban ranch house for Krystle and Blake in *Dynasty: The Reunion*. Even when the couple dances together at the end in their newly regained ballroom, we can tell that the eighties are over because the house remains unfurnished. The new *Met Home* also reminded me of when Ecumena took over St. Eligius, postmodernized the nurses' desk, and installed mauve carpeting so that the once–poverty stricken St. Eligius came to resemble the yuppie quarters of the Los Angeles doctors on *Heartbeat*. The difference was that *St. Elsewhere*, possibly the finest television program of the decade, was being (unsuccessfully, of course) yuppified, whereas *Met Home* was being de-yuppified.

Looking at American television in 1994, the eighties do appear to have been a golden age, especially since most of eighties programming is still available in the form of syndicated reruns on Lifetime or f/x. Watching *Dynasty* reruns on f/x alongside Aaron Spelling's newest hit, *Melrose Place*, in summer reruns on Fox, it is hard not to long for the mise-en-scène and intergenerational campiness of the older show. And it is hard not to notice that both broadcast services are owned by Fox, that I'm not watching anything on the old networks this summer.

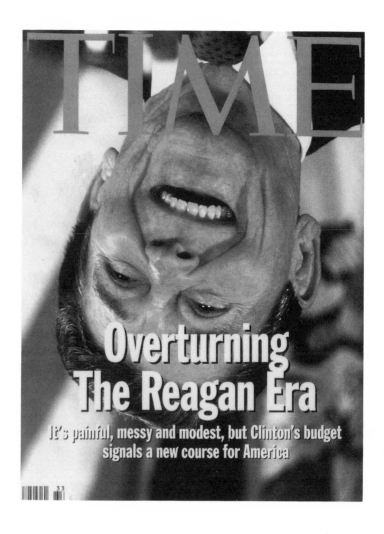

*It's painful, messy and modest, but Clinton's budget
signals a new course for America*

Could it be that the same things that made eighties TV fascinating and
contradictory politically made it fascinating and contradictory aesthetically as well?

To put it another way, postmodern TV may have represented the
best of postmodern art as an "oppositional" discourse to Reaganism,
but an oppositional discourse that was also economically dependent
on Reaganomics and in many ways complicit with Reaganite ideologies. As a form of "oppositional" discourse, it interrogated Reaganism
while drawing on the Reagan era's economic resources. And yet in
many instances, eighties TV was able to reach a mass audience unimag-
inable to the avant-garde.

In the 1970s, film theorists in France and Great Britain made a clear distinction between two kinds of cinema that could be considered counterhegemonic: the Sirkian Hollywood cinema of the fifties, riddled with "cracks and gaps" that exposed its ideological complicity, and the avant-garde independent "counter" cinema that was representationally and therefore politically pure. I wonder if an attempt to further historicize the complicitously critical fifties branch of this equation might not have revealed forces of hegemony and opposition at work similar to the ones described in this book. In the long run, I believe that the impure works will be the ones that retain aesthetic interest. That is why I have been interested in this book in deconstructing three sets of opposing terms that have structured leftist discourses around Reaganism and around television: populist/elitist, complicity/critique, and commodity/art.

Appendix A

Trauma Dramas

The starred titles were videotaped and viewed by the author. Other titles I was not able to locate but included based on summaries in reference sources. My main reference source was the excellent Alvin H. Marill (1987), *Movies Made for Television: The Telefeature and the Mini-Series: 1964–1986.*

1979

The Child Stealer. 9 March. The law won't help a young mother get her children back from her former husband.

Friendly Fire.* (Discussed in text.) 22 April.

Mrs. R.'s Daugher. 19 September. When the judicial process breaks down, a woman takes the law into her own hands to trail her daughter's rapist.

1981

Bitter Harvest.* 18 May. "Real-life story of a young farmer's efforts to find out what's killing his dairy herd and afflicting his infant son are hampered by the foot-dragging of state agricultural officials" (Marill 1987).

Broken Promise. 5 May. A juvenile court services director battles the odds to place siblings together despite bureaucratic opposition.

The Marva Collins Story.* 1 December. A Chicago schoolteacher works outside of the system to help black children. Based on a 1979 *60 Minutes* segment.

Thornwell.* 28 January. Also based on a 1979 *60 Minutes* segment. Anti–U.S. Army.

A Matter of Life and Death.* 31 January. Inspired by a 1978 *60 Minutes* segment. A nurse defies the hospital bureaucracy to aid terminally ill patients in an unconventional program.

1982

Lois Gibbs and the Love Canal.* 17 February. An ordinary housewife becomes a community activist in efforts to relocate families threatened by chemical dumping.

1983

M.A.D.D. (Mothers Against Drunk Drivers).* (Discussed in text.) 14 March.

Adam.* 10 October.

The Day After.* 20 November.

1984

With Intent to Kill. 24 October. A father sets out to put a teenage boy in jail for killing his daughter and copping an insanity plea.

*The Burning Bed.** (Discussed in text.)

*Victims for Victims.** (Discussed in text.)

*Something about Amelia.** Incest.

1985

*Toughlove.** (Discussed in text.)

*An Early Frost.** (Discussed in text.)

*Do You Remember Love?**

*The Rape of Richard Beck.** 27 May. A macho police officer confronts the indifference of the system after he himself is raped; he seeks help from a rape crisis self-help organization.

Letting Go. Features a self-help group.

*Surviving.** Teen suicide disrupts a family.

Streets of Justice. An auto worker turns vigilante to hunt down the killers of his wife and son who got off on legal loopholes.

*Children of the Night.** The real-life story of a doctoral researcher who started a halfway house for prostitutes.

1986

*Kate's Secret.** Bulimia.

*Child's Cry.** A social worker investigates a child abuse case.

*Unnatural Causes.** (Discussed in text.)

*Adam: His Song Continues.**

Many Happy Returns. Comic treatment, anti-IRS.

*A Fight for Jenny.** 6 October. An interracial child-custody battle.

*One Terrific Guy.** Child abuse by a teacher.

*Acceptable Risks.**

Resting Place. An army officer fights for the burial of a black Vietnam hero in an all-white Georgia town.

Vengeance: The Story of Tony Cimo. Tired of waiting for the courts to act, a man takes the law into his own hands and has his parents' killer killed.

Penalty Phase. A judge wrestles with the moral dilemma of whether to risk losing his family and reelection by exposing a technical flaw that would set free a mass murderer.

1987

*Right to Die.** 12 October.

*Kids like These.** 8 November.

*Mercy or Murder.** The audience decides the validity of the mercy killing of a wife with Alzheimer's by her husband.

*Baby Girl Scott.** Parents fight the bureaucracy to let their infant die in a neonatal intensive-care unit.

1988

*God Bless the Child.** 21 March.

*My Father, My Son.** Agent Orange.

*Shootdown.** Angela Lansbury gives a standout performance as a bereaved, angry mother in the wake of the 1983 downing of Korean Air Flight 007 by a Soviet fighter (description from *TV Guide*).

*To Heal a Nation.** 29 May. The true story of a vet who fought for the Vietnam Veterans' Memorial.

The Ann Jillian Story

Appendix B

Yuppie Programs

Dates given are for broadcasts of original episodes.

Hill Street Blues (15 January 1981–19 May 1987)
St. Elsewhere (26 October 1982–25 May 1988)
Miami Vice (16 September 1984–26 July 1989)
Moonlighting (3 March 1985–14 May 1989)
Hometown (22 August 1985–15 October 1985)
Jack and Mike (16 September 1986–28 May 1987)
Kay O'Brien (25 September 1986–13 November 1986)
L.A. Law (3 October 1986–19 May 1994)
Max Headroom (31 March 1987–16 October 1987)
The Days and Nights of Molly Dodd (21 May 1987–29 June 1988;
       new episodes on Lifetime cable network from 1989 to 1991)
A Year in the Life (24 August 1987–20 April 1988)
thirtysomething (29 September 1987–29 May 1991)
The Wonder Years (15 March 1988–12 May 1993)
Heartbeat (23 March 1988–6 April 1989)
China Beach (26 April 1988–22 July 1991)
Tattingers (26 October 1988–26 April 1989)

References

Advertising Age. 1988. April 11, p. S22.

———. 1989. February 20. Lifetime ad, p. 21.

Allen, Robert C. 1985. *Speaking of Soap Operas.* Chapel Hill: University of North Carolina Press.

Altman, Rick. 1987. Television Sound. In Horace Newcomb, ed., *Television: The Critical View.* 4th ed. New York: Oxford University Press.

American Demographics. 1985. The Big Chill (Revisited) or Whatever Happened to the Baby Boom? *American Demographics* 7 (Sept.): 22–29.

Arlen, Michael J. 1969. *The Living-Room War.* New York: Viking Press.

———. 1974. The Media Dreams of Norman Lear. In *The View from Highway 1.* New York: Farrar, Strauss & Giroux.

Bacon-Smith, Camille. 1992. *Enterprising Women: Television Fandom and the Creation of Popular Myth.* Philadelphia: University of Pennsylvania Press.

Baudrillard, Jean. 1983a. In the Shadow of the Silent Majorities . . . , or, the End of the Social. In Paul Foss, Paul Patton, and John Johnston, trans., *In the Shadow of the Silent Majorities and Other Essays.* New York: Semiotexte.

———. 1983b. *Simulations.* New York: Semiotexte.

Benayoun, Robert. 1986. *The Films of Woody Allen.* New York: Harmony Books.

Bennett, Tony. 1983. Texts, Readers, Reading Formations. The *Bulletin of the Midwest Modern Language Association* 16 (spring).

Bennett, Tony, and Woollacott, Janet. 1987. *Bond and Beyond: The Political Career of a Popular Hero.* New York: Methuen.

Blumenthal, Sidney. 1988. Reaganism and the Neokitsch Aesthetic. In Sidney Blumenthal and Thomas Byrne Edsall, eds., *The Reagan Legacy.* New York: Pantheon.

Brecht, Bertolt. 1979, originally 1930. The Modern Theater Is the Epic Theater. In John Willett, ed. and trans., *Brecht on Theatre.* New York: Hill and Wang.

Brode, Douglas. 1991. *The Films of Woody Allen.* New York: Carol Publishing Group.

Brooks, Peter. 1976. *The Melodramatic Imagination.* New Haven: Yale University Press.

Brooks, Tim, and Marsh, Earle. 1988. *The Complete Directory to Prime Time Network TV Shows, 1946–Present.* 4th ed. New York: Ballantine.

Browne, Nick. 1987. The Political Economy of the Television (Super) Text. In Horace Newcomb, ed., *Television: The Critical View.* 4th ed. New York: Oxford University Press.

Budge, Belinda. 1989. Joan Collins and the Wilder Side of Women. In Lorraine Gamman and Margaret Marshment, eds., *The Female Gaze: Women as Viewers of Popular Culture*. Seattle: The Real Comet Press.

Catalog Age 1992. 9:4 (April).

Choreography by George Balanchine: A Catalogue of Works. 1984. New York: Viking Press.

Davidson, Sara. 1977. *Loose Change*. Garden City, N.Y.: Doubleday.

———. 1980. *Real Property*. Garden City, N.Y.: Doubleday.

Delli Carpini, Michael X. 1986. *Stability and Change in American Politics: The Coming of Age of the Generation of the 1960s*. New York: New York University Press.

Delli Carpini, Michael, and Sigelman, Lee. 1986. Do Yuppies Matter? Competing Explanations of Their Political Distinctiveness. *Public Opinion Quarterly* 50:4 (winter): 502–518.

Dyer, Richard. 1986. *Heavenly Bodies: Film Stars and Society*. New York: BFI/Macmillan.

Edgerton, Gary. 1985. The American Made-for-TV Movie. In Brian Rose, ed., *TV Genres: A Handbook and Reference Guide*. Westport, Conn.: Greenwood Press, 1985.

Ehrenreich, Barbara. 1989. The Yuppie Strategy. In *Fear of Falling: The Inner Life of the Middle Class*. New York: Harper Collins.

Ehrenreich, Barbara, and Ehrenreich, John. 1979. The Professional-Managerial Class. In Pat Walker, ed., *Between Labor and Capital*. Boston: South End Press.

Fennimore, James. 1989. Cable Nibbling at TV's Ad Pie. *Variety*, June 28.

Feuer, Jane. 1983. The Concept of Live TV. In E. Ann Kaplan, ed., *Regarding Television*, 12–22. The American Film Institute Monograph Series, Frederick, Md.: University Publications of America.

———. 1984. Melodrama, Serial Form and Television Today. *Screen* 25 (Jan.–Feb.): 4–16.

Finch, Mark. 1986. Sex and Address in "Dynasty." *Screen* 27 (Nov.–Dec.).

Fiske, John. 1987. *Television Culture*. London: Methuen.

Foucault, Michel. 1979. What Is an Author? *Screen* 20 (spring).

Frith, Simon. 1988. Afterword: Making Sense of Video. In *Music for Pleasure*. Oxford: Polity Press.

Frith, Simon, and Horne, Howard. 1987. *Art into Pop*. London: Methuen.

Girgus, Sam B. 1993. *The Films of Woody Allen*. Cambridge University Press.

Gitlin, Todd. 1980. *The Whole World Is Watching: Mass Media in the Making and Unmaking of the New Left*. Berkeley: University of California Press.

———. 1983. *Inside Prime Time*. New York: Pantheon.

———. 1987. We Build Excitement: Car Commericals and *Miami Vice*. In Todd Gitlin, ed., *Watching Television*. New York: Pantheon.

Goodwin, Andrew. 1992. *Dancing in the Distraction Factory: Music Television and Popular Culture*. Minneapolis: University of Minnesota.

Goodwyn, Lawrence. 1978. *The Populist Moment*. New York: Oxford.

Gottlieb, Annie. 1987. *Do You Believe in Magic?: The Second Coming of the Sixties Generation*. New York: Times Books.

Greene, Bob. 1983. Jerry Rubin's New Business Is Business. *Chicago Tribune*, March 23, p. 5.

Guthrie, Lee. 1978. *Woody Allen: A Biography*. New York: Drake Publishers.

Hall, Stuart (1988). *The Hard Road to Renewal: Thatcherism and the Crisis of the Left.* London: Verso.

Hayward, Philip. 1990. How ABC Capitalised on Cultural Logic: The *Moonlighting* Story. In Manuel Alvarado and John O. Thompson, eds., *The Media Reader.* London: British Film Institute.

Heller, Leonard. 1994. Telephone conversation with the author on June 1.

Hertzberg, Hendrik. 1988. The Short Happy Life of the American Yuppie. *Esquire,* February, p. 101.

Hirsch, Foster. 1981. *Love, Sex, Death and the Meaning of Life: Woody Allen's Comedy.* New York: McGraw-Hill.

Hoban, Phoebe. 1988. All in the Family: TV's *thirtysomething* Hits Home. *New York,* February 29.

Hoke-Kahwaty, Donna. 1990. *Soap Opera Digest* 15:24 (Dec. 11): 24-29.

Hutcheon, Linda. 1986-87. The Politics of Postmodernism: Parody and History. *Cultural Critique* 5 (winter): 179-208.

———. 1989. *The Politics of Postmodernism.* London: Routledge.

Jacobs, Diane. 1982. *But We Need The Eggs: The Magic of Woody Allen.* New York: St. Martin's Press.

Jameson, Fredric. 1981. *The Political Unconscious.* Ithaca, N.Y.: Cornell University Press.

———. 1984. Postmodernism, or the Cultural Logic of Late Capitalism. *New Left Review* July–August, p. 146.

———. 1988. *The Ideologies of Theory.* Vol. 2. *Essays 1971–1986.* Minneapolis: University of Minnesota Press.

———. 1991. *Postmodernism, or, The Cultural Logic of Late Capitalism.* Durham: Duke University Press.

Jeffords, Susan. 1994. *Hard Bodies: Hollywood Masculinity in the Reagan Era.* New Brunswick, N.J.: Rutgers University Press.

Jenkins, Henry. 1992. *Textual Poachers: Television Fans and Participatory Culture.* New York: Routledge.

Johnson, Haynes. 1991. *Sleepwalking through History: America in the Reagan Years.* New York: W. W. Norton and Company.

Jones, Landon. 1980. *Great Expectations: America and the Baby Boom Generation.* New York: Ballantine Books.

Joyrich, Lynne. 1988. All That Television Allows: TV Melodrama, Postmodernism and Consumer Culture. *Camera Obscura* 16: 129-154.

Kaplan, E. Ann. 1987. *Rocking around the Clock.* London: Methuen.

Kaplan, James. 1988. The 'thirtysomething' Sell. *Manhattan, Inc.* 5 (Dec.).

Kellner, Douglas. 1989. *Jean Baudrillard.* Palo Alto: Stanford University Press.

Klein, Joe. 1985. The Real Star of *Dynasty. New York,* September 2.

Lachenbruch, David. 1990. Television in the '90s: The Shape of Things to Come. *TV Guide,* January 20.

Landy, Marcia. 1986. Culture and Politics in the Work of Antonio Gramsci. *boundary* 2, 14:3 (spring).

Lantos, Jeffrey. 1987. Talking 'Bout My Generation. *American Film,* November.

Lax, Eric. 1991. *Woody Allen: A Biography.* New York: Knopf.

Light, Paul C. 1988. *Baby Boomers.* New York: W. W. Norton and Company.

Los Angeles Times. 1985. February 10, p. 6.

MacDonald, J. Fred. 1990. *One Nation under Television: The Rise and Decline of Network TV*. New York: Pantheon.

Marchand, Roland. 1985. *Advertising the American Dream*. Berkeley: University of California Press.

Marill, Alvin H. 1987. *Movies Made for Television: The Telefeature and the Mini-Series: 1964–1986*. New York: Baseline Books.

Mayne, Judith. 1988. *L.A. Law* and Prime-Time Feminism. *Discourse*, Spring–Summer.

McCann, Graham. 1990. *Woody Allen: New Yorker*. New York: Polity.

Minsky, Terri. 1987. Yuppievision. *Rolling Stone*, December 3, pp. 41–42.

Modleski, Tania. 1982. *Loving with a Vengeance: Mass Produced Fantasies for Women*. Hamden, Conn.: The Shoe String Press.

Navacelle, Thierry de. 1987. *Woody Allen on Location*. New York: Morrow.

Nehamas, Alexander. 1990. Serious Watching. *SAQ* 89:1 (winter): 176–177.

New York. 1984. August 6, p. 15.

New York Times. 1984a. March 15, sec 3, p. 29.

———. 1984b. November 20, sec 3, p. 15.

Newsweek. 1984a. The Year of the Yuppie. *Newsweek*, December 31.

———. 1984b. They Live to Buy. *Newsweek*, December 31.

Nielsen Media Research. 1990. Data provided to the author.

Nowell-Smith, Geoffrey. 1977. Minnelli and Melodrama. *Screen* 18:2 (summer).

Orr, Christopher. 1980. Closure and Containment: Marylee Hadley in *Written on the Wind*. *Wide Angle* 4(2): 28–35.

PC Week. 1988. Upscale Lotus Software Sits Well with the BMWs on TV's *thirtysomething* [editorial]. *PC Week*, February 9, p. 32.

Peele, Gillian. 1984. *Revival and Reaction: The Right in Contemporary America*. Oxford: Clarendon Press.

People. 1984. December 17, p. 69.

Pfeil, Fred. 1990. Makin' Flippy Floppy: Postmodernism and the Baby-Boom PMC. In *Another Tale to Tell: Politics and Narrative in Postmodern Culture*. London: Verso.

Phillips, Kevin. 1983. *Post-Conservative America*. New York: Vintage Books.

Piesman, Marissa. 1993. Interview with author, Pittsburgh.

Piesman, Marissa, and Hartley, Marilee. 1984. *The Yuppie Handbook*. New York: Pocket Books.

Pogel, Nancy. 1987. *Woody Allen*. Boston: Twayne.

Pollan, Michael. 1982. The Season of the Reagan Rich. *Channels of Communication*, November–December, 2.

———. 1985. The "Vice" Look. *Channels* 5:4 (July–Aug.).

Porter, Dennis. 1977. Soap Time: Thoughts on a Commodity Art Form. *College English* 38.

Pratt, Mary Louise. 1986. Interpretive Strategies/Strategic Interpretations: On Anglo-American Reader-Response Criticism. In Jonathan Arac, ed., *Postmodernism and Politics*. Minneapolis: University of Minnesota Press.

Press, Andrea. 1990. Class, Gender and the Female Viewer: Women's Responses to *Dynasty*. In Mary Ellen Brown, ed., *Television and Women's Culture*. London: Sage.

Probyn, Elspeth. 1990. New Traditionalism And Post-Feminism: TV Does The Home. *Screen* 31(2).

Propp, Vladimir. 1968. *Morphology of the Folktale*. Trans. Laurence Scott. 2d ed. Austin: University of Texas Press.

Rabinovitz, Lauren. 1992. Soap Opera Bridal Fantasies. *Screen* 33:3 (autumn).

Radway, Janice. 1984. *Reading the Romance*. Chapel Hill: University of North Carolina Press.

Rizzo, Tony. 1985. West Coast Reporting. *Soap Opera Digest*, July 16.

Rosenberg, Howard. 1988. *Los Angeles Times*, February 29.

Ross, Andrew. 1990. Techno-Ethics and Tele-Ethics: Three Lives in the Day of Max Headroom. In Patricia Mellencamp, ed., *Logics of Television*. Bloomington: Indiana University Press.

Russell, Cheryl. 1988. Question: What Do You Call a Yuppie Stockbroker? *American Demographics*, January.

Schatz, Thomas. 1983. *Old Hollywood/New Hollywood: Ritual, Art and Industry*. Ann Arbor: UMI Research Press.

Schiff, Stephen. 1984. What *Dynasty* Says about America. *Vanity Fair*, December.

Schudson, Michael. 1978. *Discovering the News: A Social History of American Newspapers*. New York: Basic Books.

Schulze, Laurie. 1990. The Made-for-TV Movie: Industrial Practice, Cultural Form, Popular Reception. In Tino Balio, ed., *Hollywood in the Age of Television*. Boston: Unwin Hyman.

Seiter, Ellen. 1982. Eco's TV Guide — the Soaps. *Tabloid* 5 (winter): 35–43.

Shapiro, Esther. 1984. *Dynasty: The Authorized Biography of the Carringtons*. New York: Doubleday.

Silverman, Debora. 1986. *Selling Culture: Bloomingdale's, Diana Vreeland, and the New Aristocracy of Taste in Reagan's America*. New York: Pantheon.

Sirk, Douglas. 1971. *Sirk on Sirk: Interviews with Jon Halliday*. London: Secker and Warburg for the British Film Institute.

Smythe, Michael. 1988. Television Is the Key to Baby Boomers' Buying. *Broadcasting*, July 4.

Soap Opera Digest. 1982. December 7.

———. 1991. March 5.

Spignesi, Stephen J. 1992. *The Woody Allen Companion*. Kansas City, Mo.: Andrews and McMeel.

Stam, Robert. 1992. *Reflexivity in Film and Literature: From Don Quixote to Jean-Luc Godard*. New York: Columbia University Press.

thirtysomething Writers. 1991. *thirtysomething stories* . New York: Pocket Books.

Thorburn, David. 1994. Television Melodrama. In Horace Newcomb, ed., *Television: The Critical View*. 5th ed. New York: Oxford.

Torres, Sasha. 1989. Melodrama, Masculinity and the Family: *thirtysomething* as Therapy. *Camera Obscura* 19.

TV Guide. 1985. How Tough Should You Get with Your Problem Teen-ager? October 12, p. 11.

———. 1987. Danger! Please Don't Mix Facts with Fiction. November 9, p. 12.

Variety. 1989. March, p. 41.

Wall Street Journal. 1984. March 23, p. 1.

———. 1986. January 23, p. 31.

Warren, Elaine. 1985. Backstage with *Dynasty. Cosmopolitan,* August, p. 182–185.

Webster, Duncan. 1988. *Looka Yonder!: The Imaginary America of Populist Culture.* New York: Comedia/Routledge.

Wernblad, Annette. 1992. *Brooklyn Is Not Expanding: Woody Allen's Comic Universe.* Rutherford, N.J.: Fairleigh Dickinson University Press.

White, Hayden. 1980. The Value of Narrativity in the Representation of Reality. In W. J. T. Mitchell, ed., *On Narrative.* Chicago: University of Chicago Press.

Willemen, Paul. 1971. Distanciation and Douglas Sirk. *Screen* 12:2 (summer): 63–67.

Williams, Raymond. 1974. *Television: Technology and Cultural Form.* New York: Schocken Books.

Wollen, Peter. 1972. Counter Cinema: *Vent d'est. Afterimage,* autumn.

Wright, Will. 1975. *Six Guns and Society: A Structural Study of the Western.* Berkeley: University of California Press.

Wurtzler, Steve. 1988. Unpublished paper on *An Early Frost* written at the University of Iowa.

Yacowar, Maurice. 1991. *Loser Take All: The Comic Art of Woody Allen.* New expanded edition (originally published in 1979). New York: Ungar.

Zurawik, David. 1991. TV Shows Tone Down Glitz Because of Recession. *Baltimore Sun,* January 9, p. 6.

Index